ADVANCE PRAISE FOR TRANSITION TO PEACE

"In my book, I described myself as an Economic Hit Man. Given Russell Faure-Brac's earlier career in the weapons industry, I would call this creative and insightful book 'Confessions of a Defense Engineer'."

John Perkins, New York Times bestselling author
of *Confessions of an Economic Hit Man*

"We live in a time of rapid change and dwindling natural resources, increasing economic instability and growing threats of international conflict. American military dominance is no longer a viable or practical insurance against war and violence. We need big, fast change – and this book shows us the first steps to getting there."

Thom Hartmann, host of
the *Thom Hartmann Program*
and best selling author
of *Unequal Protection* and
Rebooting the American Dream

"The path to increased human happiness and an end to destructive wars is explored sincerely and passionately in Russ Faure-Brac's book *Transition to Peace*. The ideas range from simple to complex, from the commonsensical to the downright radical. You may not agree with everything that Russ says, but you will find much of value to consider. What we all agree is that we must find more sensible and sustainable ways to address our greatest conflicts. We must also do it without the horrific cost in life and resources that has been our legacy of the past. I invite you to consider Russ' ideas and join the search."

Jack Hoban,
former US Marine Corps Captain
and founder of the *Marine Corps
Martial Arts Program*

"The 21st century will be filled with conflict flash-points as nations struggle for access to diminishing resources. There is also a near-certainty of increasing domestic unrest as national economies contract. It will be a challenging time even in the best-case scenario. If we fight over the crumbs of the waning industrial era, our prospects are worse than dreary. But that need not be our fate: the social technologies on nonviolence and peacemaking are fully developed and ready to ease our transition to a world of lower consumption and greater equity.

Russ Faure-Brac has done an immense service to us all by exploring the challenges of our time and the potential for peacemaking in a book filled with clarity, compassion and insight."

Richard Heinberg, Ph.D.,
Senior Fellow at the Post Carbon Institute
and author of *The End of Growth*

"In this thoughtful book, Russell Faure-Brac just about outlines all the steps that would have to be taken to convert the United States safely from its 'permanent war economy' – and political culture – to one of peace. He describes instances of nonviolence in the face of severe opposition, the emergence of a global peaceforce (usually called Unarmed Civilian Peacekeeping) and the economic and policy changes we shall have to make if we are truly to 'rid mankind of the scourge of war.'

The hard part in these proposals is always how to get people to accept these changes; but surely 'hard' becomes impossible if they do not have what historian Arnold Toynbee called 'a practical, intelligible plan' for realizing such a grand idea. That is where the comprehensive proposals in this book could be of great help."

Michael Nagler, Ph.D.,
President of the Metta Center for Nonviolence
and author of *The Search for a Nonviolent Future*.

"Russ Faure-Brac has joined the ranks of workers for war who turn creatively to work for peace. Both war and peace workers can benefit greatly from this book."

Glenn Paige, Ph.D.,
Chair, Governing Council of the Center for Global Nonkilling
and author of *Nonkilling Global Political Science*

"Russell Faure-Brac writes that he's 'just a regular guy, writing for regular people.' Yet our future depends on fulfilling the kind of deep quest that Russell is engaged in, searching for a transition to peace. With an open heart and a discerning mind, he has pursued a winding path of the sort that will be essential for the survival of humanity and in fact for life on this planet.

All of us have found ourselves at crossroads of pain and hope, obstacles and opportunities to move beyond what Martin Luther King, Jr. called the 'madness of militarism.' In *Transition to Peace*, Russell Faure-Brac challenges himself – and all of us – to set aside easy answers and explore where a road to peace might take us. The journey beckons and this book can help us find our way."

Norman Solomon,
author of *War Made Easy:*
How Presidents and Pundits Keep Spinning Us to Death

"As globalization and economic growth are hitting limits, this book makes the case that peace is achievable, given the rapidly changing nature of our world. Russell Faure-Brac offers a unique and compelling prescription for a new national security policy and a challenge for today's leaders and citizens to create a more peaceful society. I highly recommend this book to all seekers of peace."

Jerry Mander,
author of *The Case Against the Global Economy*
and *The Capitalism Papers: Six Fatal Flaws of an Obsolete System*

TRANSITION TO PEACE

A Defense Engineer's Search for an Alternative to War

Russell Faure-Brac

OPEN BOOK
EDITIONS
A Berrett–Koehler Partner

Transition to Peace
A Defense Engineer's Search for an Alternative to War

iUniverse books may be ordered through booksellers or by contacting:

iUniverse
1663 Liberty Drive
Bloomington, IN 47403
www.iuniverse.com
1-800-Authors (1-800-288-4677)

ISBN: 978-1-4697-3078-3 (sc)
ISBN: 978-1-4697-3077-6 (hc)
ISBN: 978-1-4697-3079-0 (e)

Library of Congress Control Number: 2012900353

Printed in the United States of America

iUniverse rev. date: 3/28/2012

Dear Mom and Les,

Mom, when I was young, you always knew how to smooth things over and bring peace to the family. When I was angry, you helped me see the other side. When I was confused, you helped me understand. When I was hurt, you soothed my wounds. You were the embodiment of your own gentle phrase, "Peace begins at home."

Les, you combined strength and gentleness in a way that few brothers do. You had a way of cheering others up with your hearty laugh, silly jokes, and enthusiasm for John Denver songs. Yet in football, you were the tough linebacker that running backs feared. Then as a Marine, you lived the horror of Vietnam, and when you returned home, you swore you would never fight again. Survivor guilt finally caught up to you after twenty-four years in the tragic ending that has afflicted so many veterans.

Thanks, Mom and Les, for being teachers of peace in my life. The whole world should have known you.

Love,

Russ

CONTENTS

Part III. How to Get There

LIST OF FIGURES

LIST OF STORIES

ACKNOWLEDGMENTS

My work on this book began during the presidency of George W. Bush and continued into the administration of Barack Obama. During that time, my thinking evolved about the subject of peace and how to get there. Initially I looked at nonviolence for the answer. While I fully embrace its concepts, it somehow seemed incomplete. How do we jump from being the powerful, militaristic nation we are today to being a force for nonviolence in the future? I then explored the idea of Peaceful Warriorship, as expressed in certain forms of martial arts, which gave clues as to how a transition to peace might take place. My various ideas began to coalesce after studying the concept of permaculture. Its principles and ethics gave me new ideas about how to restructure our defense posture.

Along the way, a number of special people opened my eyes to these and other concepts and inspired me to dig deeper for answers. First, I want to thank Michael Nagler, the UC Berkeley scholar and longtime peace advocate, and Arun Gandhi, grandson of Mahatma Gandhi, for sharing their ideas about the role of nonviolence in seeking sustainable peace. I am deeply grateful to Jack Hoban, Joe Lau, and Dr. Richard Strozzi-Heckler, all degree holders in aikido, jujutsu, or other martial arts, who showed me how compassion can be combined with physical skills.

I thank permaculture instructors Penny Livingston and James Stark, who showed me that by sticking my hands in the soil, I could discover principles for living peacefully on the planet. Mark Zaifman and I spent many hours discussing the state of the American economy and how peace is ultimately a pocketbook issue. I thank him for parting the veil on the mysterious science of economics. Many thanks go to Glenn Paige for the time we spent in Honolulu talking about his concept of nonkilling.

Thanks go to reviewers of the first draft of the book, including Norman Solomon, Beth and Scott Wachenheim, Sadja Greenwood, Alan Margolis, and the late Jonathan Rowe. For producing the book, many thanks go to the editorial and production staff of Open Book Editions. And thanks to graphics designer Mariah Parker, who turned my rough sketches into a professional product.

Most importantly, I want to thank my family. Gabe and Josh relentlessly challenged my ideas and helped me see things through the eyes of a younger generation. My brother Mike kept my humor up when I was reading story after depressing story about mankind's shortcomings. And finally I want to thank my wife, Anne Sands, the radiant light of my life, who encouraged me all the way and endured my search for an alternative to war.

INTRODUCTION

WHILE THE VIETNAM WAR was raging, I was in my office fiddling with a slide rule, calculating the most cost-effective way to blow up the world. It was 1967, and I was part of the military-industrial-think tank complex, working for Stanford Research Institute (now SRI International) as a systems analyst. I didn't think war made any sense, but as with most people, I believed we had to live with it as a necessary evil. Besides, I wasn't carrying a rifle on the front lines—I was just doing technically interesting work behind the scenes with a defense deferment, compliments of the Selective Service System.

One day, I found myself staring at a top-secret map of radar and missile installations in North Vietnam. My job was to analyze the use of electronic countermeasures (ECM) equipment by our naval strike aircraft to determine the best way to penetrate past North Vietnamese radar and missile sites. The data from this analysis would assist the Department of Defense (DOD) in making purchase decisions for ECM devices in the future. In doing the calculations, I remember using the term p(k), meaning the probability of kill, and placing a dollar value on the loss of an American soldier's life (about $50,000 then). No accounting was made for the value of Vietnamese lives.

That was when I went over the edge—my defining moment. I couldn't believe it had to be this way; there had to be an alternative to the craziness of war. But I felt I couldn't quit my job unless I believed there was a viable alternative to war. So I started taking classes at the Institute for the Study of Nonviolence and studied the principles and actions of Gandhi, Martin Luther King, and others.

I participated in a role-playing exercise called Peace Games, exploring the concept of nonviolent civil resistance against an invading Russian army. I also attended the Tuesday luncheons of a support group for disillusioned people working in the defense industry.

After a year of study, I concluded that war was not a necessary evil and that there was a more effective and sane way to defend ourselves. In an act of youthful defiance, I hung a poster in my office saying "War is not healthy for children and other living things." Shortly thereafter, my supervisor tore it down, saying, "It would offend our clients."

I sought in vain for nondefense work in the company (90 percent of our contracts at the time came from the DOD), and then I decided to resign. Most of us have a major turning point in our lives, and that was mine. Determined to place an exclamation mark on my decision, I made a film called *But What Do We Do?* documenting my decision to leave the defense industry.

I then began a career as an environmental planner, in which I mostly forgot about issues of war and peace. Thirty years later, after selling my business and retiring, I watched the World Trade Center towers collapse in the attacks of 9/11. It triggered memories of my earlier years grappling with the question of war. It was an opportunity to revisit my earlier beliefs and to delve into the issue more deeply. How, specifically, could our nation, so invested in war, find a path to peace? That was the genesis of this book.

Definition of Peace
There are many definitions of peace, some more useful than others. At the very least, peace is not just an absence of war, nor is it forcibly imposed. My definition of peace is: an ideal state in which justice prevails and methods other than war are used to resolve international conflict.

This definition underscores the point that peace is not an end state but rather an ongoing process of moving in that direction. It requires that justice be present, as true peace cannot exist in an unjust society. And the definition leaves open the ways in which peace can be pursued without going to war. There's not a rigid divide between peace and no peace. It's more a question of how far we can move on a continuum from total war toward total peace.

An Impossible Dream?

You may believe that peace is an impossible, naive dream; it is counter to human nature and there are too many political, economic, and cultural obstacles to overcome. But cooperation and compassion, in addition to competition and violence, are also part of the human condition. We have the capacity for both and the ability to choose either.

Furthermore, we appear to be entering a transformative time where very large changes in societal structure will rapidly occur, whether by choice, by circumstances we have created, or by forces that are out of our control. Whether we move in a direction toward peace or continue the old ways of war is up to us.

Whether peace is possible or not, you may believe that American economic and military domination of the globe is a good thing. It has served us well in the past, and those who have the power deserve the rewards. But other countries such as China and India will soon be overtaking us economically, if they haven't already. Being a military superpower is no guarantee of continuing domination, as we have seen in the failed empires of history.

I realize that my ideas are unconventional. But the research I have done convinces me that believing in peace is realistic. It's all a question of how we look at things. Once we believe that peace is possible, we can then act to bring it about. The process will be messy, and things will have to get worse, probably much worse, before they can get better. But ultimately I believe that we can and will create a more peaceful future.

Three Questions

This is not an academic treatise, nor am I an expert on the subject of war and peace. I'm just a regular guy, writing for regular people. While I borrow generously from others' proposals, I combine their ideas with those of my own in perhaps a unique way. I also cover some topics that may seem unrelated to peace, but everything is connected to everything else in this world, and the path to peace may take some unusual routes.

You might be surprised that you are reading such outlandish information. Perhaps you are a lifelong Republican who despises Democrats, because you see them as soft and weak on fighting terrorism, or maybe you're a left wing progressive who has attended every antiwar march since Vietnam and who blames right wing conservatives for everything that's wrong with this country. Or perhaps your sixteen-year-old daughter just gave you this book to read, and you're wondering what's in it.

However this information reaches your hands, I pose three questions to you and to all Americans who want a better and more secure life for themselves, their family, and their country.

- Does our current defense system make you feel safe?
- Is it worth the cost?
- Is there an alternative to war, and can you help make it happen?

Whether you have your answers to these questions or are unsure of where you stand, let's explore together the issue of world peace and how to get there.

Russell Faure-Brac

PART I

Where We Are

1. REFLECTIONS ON WAR

If you wish for peace, understand war.
—*Sir Basil Liddell Hart, military historian*

THERE ARE MANY THINGS to be said about war: its glory and horrors, its causes and effects, and whether there is such a thing as a "just war." Of all the aspects of war, I'm not going to address the most obvious ones. Rather, I want to focus on just a few points that struck me the most in my research and that seem most relevant to this discussion.

Major American Wars

For centuries, nations have used war as their primary tool to provide for security and common defense. The United States is no exception, having participated in our share of conflict, perhaps more than we realize. Since our founding, we have engaged in fourteen major wars, an average of one every seventeen years as shown in Figures 1 & 2. This does not include sixty-five smaller incursions such as the 1961 Bay of Pigs invasion, the 1989 invasion of Panama, the 1995 intervention in Bosnia-Herzegovina, and ongoing Central Intelligence Agency (CIA) covert operations from 1947 to the present. No political party has had a corner on the war market. Of all the presidencies in our country's history, major wars have been fought under both Democratic administrations (sixteen) and Republican (fifteen).

History of Major American Wars		
Date	**Name**	**President**
1775-1783	American Revolutionary War	George Washington (Unaffiliated)
1812-1815	War of 1812	James Madison (Democratic-Republican)
1817-1891	American Indian Wars	7 Democrats, 6 Republicans, 7 Other
1846-1848	Mexican-American War	James K. Polk (D)
1861-1865	American Civil War	Abraham Lincoln (R)
1898	Spanish-American War	William McKinley (R)
1899-1913	Philippine-American War	McKinley (R), T. Roosevelt (R), Taft (R)
1917-1918	World War I	Woodrow Wilson (D)
1941-1945	World War II (1941-1945)	F. D. Roosevelt (D), Harry S. Truman (D)
1950-1953	Korean War	Harry S. Truman (D)
1962-1975	Vietnam War	Kennedy (D), Johnson (D), Nixon (R)
1991-1992	Persian Gulf War	George H. W. Bush (R)
2001-Present	Afghanistan War	George W. Bush (R), Barack Obama (D)
2003-Present	Iraq War	George W. Bush (R), Barack Obama (D)

Source: New York Public Library Desk Reference, Third Edition

Figure 1. History of major American wars. Note that wars have been fought equally by both Democratic and Republican administrations.

Sometimes as a nation, we felt war was justified (World War II), in some cases we concluded that the war was a mistake (Vietnam), and sometimes our involvement was highly questionable (Iraq). There were even times when we weren't sure why we were there (World War I). Regardless, war has been a steady part of the American experience.

US Military Bases
We have a large network of military bases at home and abroad—about 500 domestic and around 1,000 foreign bases. They range from small outposts to bustling military cities. As an example of how big our foreign bases can be, the Victory Base Complex in Baghdad

housed more than 100,000 military personnel and contractors during the Iraq War.

Few other countries have any foreign military bases. Even China, with the world's second largest military budget, has no foreign bases, although it may be forced to change its policy by the ramping up of US bases in the Asia-Pacific region. No foreign country, of course, has any military bases on American soil.

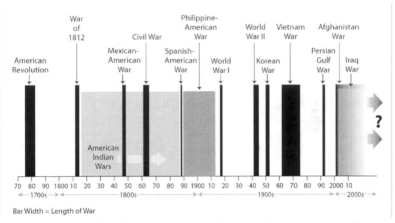

Figure 2. Timeline of American wars. The United States has engaged in major wars on average once every seventeen years.

In the Mideast, where two thirds of the world's oil reserves are located, we have twenty-six strategically located air bases as shown in Figure 3. While they are there to ensure our access to oil, their presence creates an interesting dynamic. Consider the situation of Iran. It is surrounded by US bases on all sides and by Afghanistan on its east and Iraq on its west, countries we invaded in 2001 and 2003, respectively. It's the equivalent of Iran surrounding the United States with twenty-six of their military bases, then invading Canada and Mexico. Is it a surprise that they want to develop a nuclear weapon?

Our military is now shifting its focus from the Mideast to Asia and the Pacific, where China is perceived as a major economic threat. Trade officials from the United States and eight Pacific Rim nations are negotiating a new Trans-Pacific Free Trade Agreement that would "facilitate a favorable and sustainable business environment" in the region. In support of its economic interests, the United States is strengthening its military presence there. We currently have military bases in Guam, Japan, South Korea, Australia, eight other South Pacific islands, and five of the seven islands of Hawaii. New permanent bases and facilities are under construction in Darwin, Australia; on the main island of Hawaii; and on Jeju Island, South Korea. The $1 billion naval facility on Jeju would base submarines and an Aegis ballistic missile defense system, serving as a forward operating base in the event of military conflict with China.

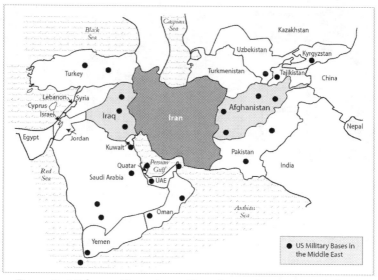

Figure 3. Mideast military bases. Note that we have surrounded Iran with military bases and invaded countries on both her east and her west.

Astronomical Cost

War is expensive. Although devilishly difficult to decipher, the total national security budget for 2012 can be calculated in the following way. The total proposed federal budget was $3.7 trillion. Of that, $1.6 trillion was for the mandatory programs of Social Security, Medicare, and Medicaid, leaving a balance of $2.1 trillion for discretionary spending. Of that remaining balance, $1.3 trillion was national security spending, which is much greater than just the base budget for DOD, once you add in all other related costs as shown in Figure 4.

2012 National Security Budget	$ Billions
DOD Base Budget	$558
Pentagon share of interest on the national debt	185
Military operations in Iraq and Afghanistan	118
Pension benefits—military and civilian	69
"Direct security spending"	18
Miscellaneous costs beyond Base Budget	8
Subtotal DOD	**956**
Veteran's Administration	129
CIA & other intelligence agencies	53
Department of Homeland Security	3
Department of Energy (nuclear weapons program)	19
State Department (counter-terrorism activities)	9
Department of Health & Human Services	5
Department of Justice	5
National security portion of other programs (NASA, Treasury Department, etc.)	8
TOTAL	**$1,294 = $1.3 Trillion**

Sources: *Budget of the US Government, Fiscal Year 2012 (Office of Management and Budget), "The Figure No One Wants You To See," Chris Hellman*

Figure 4. 2012 US national security budget. The money we spend on national security is far greater than just the Department of Defense base budget.

Story 1. What's a Trillion?

Million, billion, and trillion sound very similar, but they are not. In terms of time:

1 million seconds = 12 days;
1 billion seconds = 32 years; and
1 trillion seconds = 32,000 years.

Convert time into money, and you get a sense of how much we are spending on national security.

The $1.3 trillion for national security spending represents 62 percent of total discretionary spending as shown in Figure 5. For those who believe that the primary function of the federal government should be defense, this

5

looks pretty good. For those who believe that government has a wider responsibility, national security takes up a disproportionate share of the budget.

Another way of looking at our defense budget is to compare it to what is spent by other countries. Figure 6 shows that the US military budget exceeds that of all the other world's military expenditures combined.

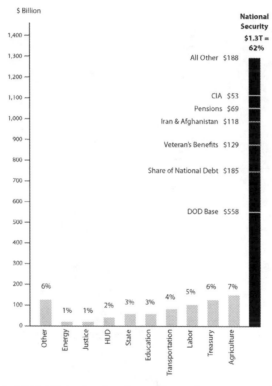

Figure 5. 2012 US budget breakout. National security spending is by far the largest part of our federal discretionary budget.

A Changing Battlefield

Modern terrorism has confounded our traditional ways of fighting war. The new battlefield is no longer uniformed armies fighting over territory, where more soldiers and better weapons lead to victory. Terrorism is leading the way to what's called asymmetric warfare, where a very small organization such as al Qaeda can inflict great damage on a very large nation such as ours.

Here at home, the best Star Wars missile defense system could not have stopped the attacks of 9/11. If there is another 9/11-type attack, it will be difficult for our military to respond. We have virtually destroyed all the physical assets of al Qaeda, and its cells are spread throughout the world, not in any one location. When we invade foreign countries, insurgents strike and blend into the surrounding population, frustrating our attempt to avoid civilian casualties. It ends up being a constant game of cat and mouse that is very difficult for us to "win." New ways of defending our country need to be developed.

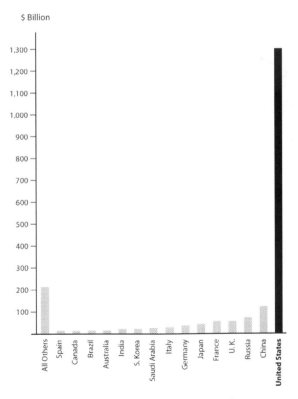

Figure 6. Military spending comparison. No other country spends anywhere near what we do on defense.

Apart from the taking of lives, terrorists are successfully waging an economic war against us. Al Qaeda's $500,000 attack of 9/11 triggered two wars and a homeland security program costing on the order of $5 trillion when everything is added up. And once we spend tons of money to increase airline and port security, terrorists can easily adopt another form of attack, forcing us to spend even more in a never-ending cycle of response. By hijacking our own planes and using inexpensive weapons like box cutters, shoe bombs, and exploding print cartridges, terrorists are economically bleeding us to death. As someone said, "We have a global nuclear navy. Al Qaeda doesn't even have a rowboat."

2. A RAPIDLY CHANGING WORLD

Predictions are always difficult, especially about the future.
—Niels Bohr, quantum physicist

THE WORLD IS CHANGING so rapidly we will hardly recognize it in twenty years. Given the world's exploding population, the impending end of cheap oil, and the effects of climate change, we are hitting limits in the Earth's carrying capacity. And our national and global economic systems are fragile and subject to breakdown. These factors have huge implications for the future mission, structure, and operation of our military system.

Overpopulation

The world's population has grown at an alarming rate over the last hundred years, soaring from 1.6 billion in 1900 to the current figure of 7 billion, with the graph shooting up exponentially, in the shape of a hockey stick, as shown in Figure. 7. The United Nations predicts that population will continue to increase rapidly, reaching a peak of 9.8 billion in 2050, less than forty years from now, assuming there is no population collapse.

If there is population collapse, it could occur in one of two ways. In the first, population implodes from world famine, thermonuclear war, or some natural disaster; clearly, an option we don't want. The second way would involve a proactive effort on the part of all nations to set a goal and implement policies to reduce population size, an action that is not likely to happen.

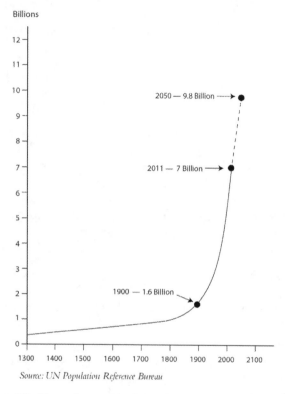

Billions

Source: UN Population Reference Bureau

Figure 7. World population. The shape of exponential population growth looks like a hockey stick.

Accompanying population growth will be increased consumption, particularly in rich countries. There is the oft-quoted statistic that the US, with 5 percent of the world's population, consumes about 25 percent of the world's resources. The growth of both population and consumption, particularly if the rest of the world attempts to achieve the US standard of living, will continue to put unprecedented pressure on the ability of the Earth to provide for our needs and absorb our wastes. Dr. Paul Erlich, professor of Population Studies at Stanford University, estimates that at the current rate of growth and consumption, total societal collapse from population pressure could occur in the next thirty to forty years (*Humanity on a Tightrope* by Paul Erlich and Robert Ornstein).

Overpopulation will create an uncertain future, in effect tossing the pieces on the chessboard into the air. As a result, our military will have to adjust and operate in a very different environment from the past.

Peak Oil

The term "peak oil" means that global oil production (extraction and refining) has reached a peak and will steadily and permanently decline in the future, until it is no longer an economically viable source of energy as shown in Figure 8. Since the first commercial oil well was drilled in Poland in 1853, oil production has increased annually, with a blip on the upswing during the 1970s Arab oil embargo. There is some disagreement as to when we hit the peak, with estimates ranging from 1990 to 2020. The International Energy Administration (IEA) says production of conventional crude oil peaked in 2006. Regardless of the exact date, we are basically at peak oil now, meaning that oil in the future will be decreasing in availability and dramatically increasing in price.

As stated by Michael Brownlee in "From Fossil Fuel Dependence to Local Resilience, One Community at a Time" (March 23, 2010, Transition Colorado):

> There are now 98 oil producing nations in the world. Sixty-four of them have already reached their peak in oil production and are in decline. That is fundamentally why oil prices have been rising so dramatically. All the low-hanging fruit has already been picked. The rest is lower quality, requires more processing, and is mostly available in very harsh environments—several miles under the bottom of the ocean, in the tar sands of the fragile Canadian tundra, or in countries not particularly friendly to the West.

At the same time, worldwide demand for oil, especially in the growing economies of China, India, and Brazil, is rapidly increasing, with the United States leading all others in per capita consumption. The net result is that we are going to run out of commercially available cheap oil, perhaps within the next forty or fifty years. We don't accept it yet, but the Oil Age will soon be over. This is vividly illustrated by the Petroleum Interval curve as shown in Figure 8, in which the Oil Age can be seen as a brief 200-year period in the Earth's history.

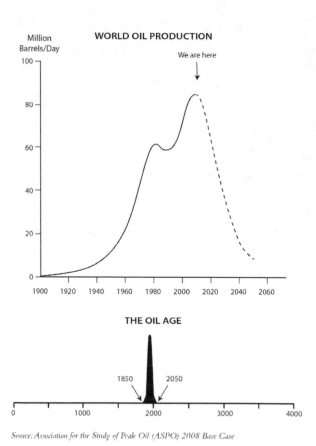

Source: Association for the Study of Peak Oil (ASPO) 2008 Base Case

Figure 8. Peak oil. Oil production has peaked and will decline rapidly in the near future.

It is true that there are ways to compensate for declining oil supplies, such as using substitute energy sources, increasing efficiency, and developing new innovative technologies. The problem is that no foreseeable alternatives are practical, affordable, or likely to be developed in time to replace oil. Substitutes may have their own "peaking" problems and constraints on how they can be applied. Increasing efficiency has a "rebound effect" where efficiency makes energy cheaper, which increases demand.

Peak oil will have a number of direct consequences on society at large:

- Increasing demand for oil and declining supplies will cause the price of oil to rise, which will stunt continued economic growth.
- Communities will have to relocalize their economies.
- Globalization will decline as oil becomes less available for transporting people, agricultural produce, and manufactured goods.
- Automobile ownership and travel will decline, affecting the auto industry and subsidiary businesses.
- Companies like Wal-mart will have to significantly change their business models as the transportation cost for goods from low-wage countries becomes increasingly prohibitive.
- Resource wars will break out as countries go after the last drop of oil. As stated by ex-Special Forces Stan Goff, "If the principle export of Iraq were palm dates, we wouldn't be there."

The implications for the military will be especially profound. The US military is the world's largest single consumer of energy and can't function in its traditional way without huge supplies of oil. As a result, the Pentagon is actively planning to "get off oil" as soon as possible.

Christine Parthemore, a fellow at the Center for New American Security, has coauthored a report recommending that the "DOD should ensure that it can operate all of its systems on nonpetroleum fuels by 2040." Navy Secretary Ray Malbus has promised that the Navy will be 50 percent oil-free by 2020, using a mix of solar, wind, geothermal, biofuels, and nuclear power. The Air Force and Navy are developing biofuels made from algae for their aircraft, vehicles, ships, and generators. And the Army is pursuing an aggressive "net zero" program for its permanent bases worldwide, so that the net production and consumption of energy, water, and waste will be zero.

However, there is a question as to how fast and how completely the technological conversions will actually occur. If there isn't enough fuel to power weapon systems or to transport personnel and equipment to the far corners of the Earth, the Pentagon will be forced to reexamine its operations. It could shift from conventional warfare and rely more on highly secret and less expensive Special Operations Forces, such as the Navy Seals. Or we could move toward a national security policy that relies more on diplomacy and "soft power" and less on military interventions. Regardless, peak oil is just one of many factors that will require our defense posture to significantly change in the future.

Climate Change
Climate change refers to a shift in global weather patterns, measured by yardsticks such as the Earth's surface temperature, wind and rainfall patterns, and the frequency of extreme weather events. The term is commonly used interchangeably with "global warming" and "the greenhouse effect," but climate change is a more accurate phrase. A major contributor and good indicator of climate change is the atmospheric concentration of carbon dioxide (CO_2). As the level of CO_2 rises, the Earth's temperature increases, causing more water to evaporate from the oceans and the land to lose water more quickly to the sky. These changes alter the dynamics of meteorological activity.

For millions of years, the levels of atmospheric CO_2 fluctuated between 180 and 280 parts per million (ppm). Then in the 1800s, CO_2 levels began to increase exponentially from around 250 ppm to over 390 ppm today as shown in Figure 9. Generally, 350 ppm is considered the safe limit to avoid irreversible, runaway climate change occurring in vicious feedback loops. The effects of climate change may represent the greatest threat ever to human civilization, including rising sea levels caused by melting ice sheets, loss of fisheries due to ocean acidification, greater frequency and magnitude of hurricanes and other severe weather events, increases in floods and droughts resulting in crop failures, and thawing permafrost, which will release methane into the atmosphere (methane is many times more potent a greenhouse gas than CO_2).

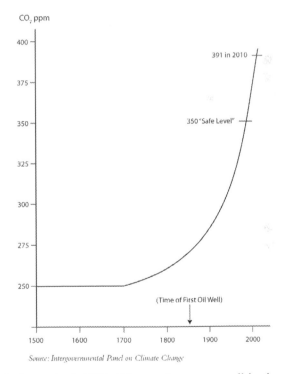

Source: Intergovernmental Panel on Climate Change

Figure 9. Atmospheric CO2. Climate change may well be the greatest threat ever to human civilization, drastically altering the world we live in.

To take one example, if sea levels rise four feet by 2100 (predicted by Rahmstorf, 2007, and Pfeffer, 2008), coastal cities around the world (London, Shanghai, Cairo, Miami, New Orleans) will be underwater and uninhabitable, creating millions of climate refugees. Two real estate markets will emerge, one in coastal areas where values plummet and the other in interior areas where prices soar. Our military is well aware of the risks, with 153 US Naval installations vulnerable to sea level rise.

There is overwhelming evidence that manmade greenhouse gasses are the major contributor to the CO_2 increase. Scientists have stated that bringing climate change under control will require that CO_2 levels level off by 2020, then decline sharply to 350 ppm. In order to achieve this goal, an ambitious plan needs to be in place by 2012. Required actions include reducing CO_2 emissions from twenty to two pounds per capita per day, no minor task. Climate change is no longer just an issue for the future. It's happening now.

Someone has said that if climate were a bank, we would have already fixed it. However, climate is not a bank, and given the inability of governments to address the problem, it is unlikely that corrective action will be taken in time. This is one more example of how our future will be very different from the past, causing our military to function in a very different world.

Economic Instability

In 2011, wild fluctuations in the stock market, continued home foreclosures, high unemployment, a near default on the US national debt, and the collapse of economies in Europe were all signs that domestic and global economies are in a state of high instability. The following are just some of the reasons for this.

Growth. The Western model of capitalism depends on perpetual economic growth (i.e., continuously increasing production and consumption of goods). But continued, unlimited growth is not possible. For most of human history, the size of the economy has been small compared to the capacity of the environment on which it depends. Over the last century, the global economy has grown so much, and the use of resources and energy has increased so dramatically, that we are now in a state of global ecological overshoot. Resources in the future will require more processing because they will be of lower quality, they will be more expensive to extract, and accessing them will be more damaging to the environment. As a result, traditional growth is beginning to hit its limits, with destabilizing economic results.

Story 3. Collapse Scenario

It is impossible to know exactly how system collapse might occur, but one can imagine. The following scenario follows an economic path.

1. Republicans in Congress won't cut defense spending or allow taxes to be increased on anybody, while Democrats won't reduce spending on needed social and infrastructure programs. Corporate lobbyists whittle back recommendations for deficit reduction. Annual deficits and national debt payments continue to increase until not enough money remains to run the country.

2. In desperation, the Federal Reserve Bank creates more money, resulting in hyperinflation and a worsening economy. The US dollar, which for decades has been the world's reserve currency (the primary currency used to transact business worldwide), loses its status and is replaced by a combination of Euros, Japanese yens, and Russian rubles. Demand for the US dollar drops precipitously, causing its devaluation and an increase in interest rates on US borrowing.

3. World markets lose confidence in the ability of the United States to govern and fear it won't repay its debts. The United States hits a global credit limit and can no longer borrow. Our government defaults on its debts and becomes essentially bankrupt, moving into a modern depression more severe than that of 1929.

4. The US economic collapse is felt globally as other countries strive desperately to keep their economies afloat. Lending countries lose the money they have "invested" in the United States. The global economy goes into a tailspin, resulting in worldwide economic collapse.

I don't know if this depressing scenario overstates the case or not, but it gives an indication of how fragile and interlinked the United States and global economies are. Think now about the effects on our military. How can it continue to function as usual if the United States runs out of money?

And it doesn't take a lack of oil or any other natural resource to bring economic growth to a halt. In 2008, a simple lack of credit caused worldwide growth to virtually cease. As a result of defaulting home loans, banks became unwilling (or unable) to lend money to individuals, corporations, or the government. When banks stop lending, the economy stops growing, and that's exactly what happened. It was only after drastic measures were taken by the Federal Reserve Bank (the Fed) and the central banks of other countries that shaky financial systems were propped up. It was a close call, illustrating the interconnected and fragile nature of the world economy.

Economic Bubbles. An economic bubble occurs when the price of a product, such as a home or a corporate stock, is sold at an increasingly inflated value. It can be difficult to know when a bubble is occurring because prices can fluctuate erratically and become impossible to predict from supply and demand theory. When the price suddenly drops, the bubble bursts. To date, there is no generally accepted explanation as to the cause of financial bubbles, although greed and denial of the product's real value are certainly factors.

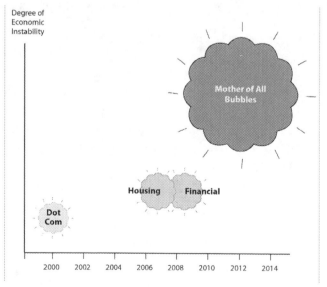

Figure 10. Economic bubbles. Global economic instability is a greater short-term threat than peak oil or climate change, which are longer acting threats.

What we do know, however, is that bubbles do happen. In *A Short History of Financial Euphoria*, Keynesian economist John Kenneth Galbraith documents that cycles of boom and bust have occurred worldwide over the last 360 years. Lately our economy has been experiencing its share. We felt the effects of three of them in the first decade of this century: the dot.com bubble in 2000, the housing bubble in 2007, followed closely by the financial market bubble of 2008. Unaltered, our economy could soon experience the Mother of All Bubbles, resulting in severe economic contraction, possible collapse, and the need to reframe our nation's economic and social structure.

National Debt. When annual government expenses exceed revenues, we incur what is called a "deficit." This requires that the government borrow money to cover the cost of running the country. When this occurs year after year, as has been happening, the amount of money our country owes, called the "national debt," increases. The problem is exacerbated when our government spends money fighting simultaneous wars and extends trillions to bail out failing banks and large corporations. The United States is now the largest debtor nation in the world, with most of our borrowing coming from China and other Asian countries. Nearly 50 percent of the debt is now leaving the country, as opposed to when interest was paid mainly to US citizens who were holding the debt.

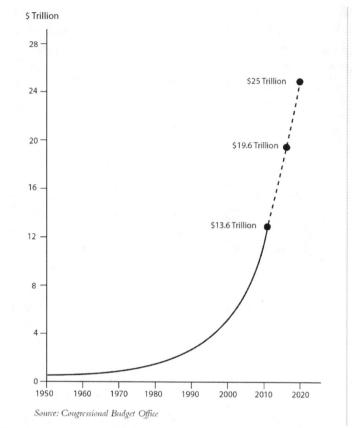

Source: *Congressional Budget Office*

Figure 11. US national debt. While short-term stimulus spending may be needed, uncontrolled national debt could cause the US and global economies to collapse.

The one thing a business cannot afford to do is run out of money; it's the same with governments. Congress seems unable to tie its own shoes, let alone control the skyrocketing national debt. As shown in Figure 11, the US national debt has risen steadily since 1980, reaching $13.6 trillion in 2010, and is projected to climb to $19.6 trillion by 2015. If the debt continues to climb this way, the interest payments alone become increasingly burdensome. While short-term stimulus spending may be needed, an uncontrolled national debt could potentially bring our economy down and the global economy with it.

Where We're Stuck

We need fast and big change, but it's hard to accept change of any pace. Change is scary, and we will deny the need for it until we are slapped in the face with the results of inaction. If we have never seen something happen before, we tend to believe that it can't and won't happen. This is especially true when politicians hide the truth, either because they don't want to scare us, because they fear the message will be politically rejected by the public, or because they want to take advantage of the short-term situation for as long as possible.

But we're well beyond the knee of the exponential curve in population, climate change, and the national debt and we're on the descending side of energy. Because exponential change cannot continue indefinitely, conventional assumptions about the future will no longer hold. Very large changes in our social and economic structure are about to occur, whether by choice, by circumstances we have created, or by forces that are out of our control. We're in an unprecedented, transformative time that is here now.

All of this has ramifications for peace. It is very unlikely that military solutions of the past will work in the future. War is astronomically and unsustainably expensive. In a time of dangerously high national debt and desperate attempts to balance the federal budget, we will not be able to continue spending on war. Given that Americans are intolerant of high taxes, inefficient government, and anything negatively affecting their pocketbook, they may rebel against a national security budget that consumes over half of all federal discretionary spending and demand a reduction in defense spending that goes far beyond belt tightening. The military can't operate without oil and money, and we're running out of both.

Time is not on our side, as Washington is strangled by its own politics. Today we're less threatened by jihadists than by the inability to get out of our own way. It's time to get unstuck and take a fresh look at our assumptions about military force leading to peace. But we're stuck because:

1. We don't know what peace is;
2. We don't believe it's possible; and
3. If it is, we don't know how to "do" it.

We clearly need a new way of thinking. Good places to start can be found in the fundamentals of nonviolence as developed by Mahatma Gandhi, the principles of warriorship as practiced in certain forms of martial arts, and the philosophy of permaculture.

PART II

Seeking Peace

3. MODELS FOR CHANGE

In the long run, nonviolence succeeds even when it fails, while violence fails even when it succeeds.
—Mahatma Gandhi

NONVIOLENCE HAS BEEN USED as a strategy for resisting injustice throughout history. While often derided as naive, outdated, and ineffective against forces such as Hitler's Germany or modern Islamic terrorists, its advantages in political conflict are largely misunderstood and underappreciated. Nonviolence, when properly applied, is an incredibly powerful force that can form the foundation for a new type of national defense.

Nonviolence

Brief History
While many people throughout the years have practiced nonviolence, Mahatma Gandhi was the inventor of its most modern form. Born in India in 1869, he eventually traveled to Britain to complete a law degree in 1891. His ideas about nonviolence first developed in South Africa, where he fought against discrimination toward Indians and successfully overturned segregation laws.

After returning to India in 1915, he began a nonviolent campaign for Indian independence, confounding the British with a force they didn't understand and couldn't defeat. The most dramatic example of his civil disobedience was the 230-mile "March to the Sea" in 1930, to illegally take salt from the ocean in defiance of the British Salt Act. Joined eventually by 70,000 supporters, he walked the entire distance, stepped into the waters of the Indian Ocean, and took a pinch of salt, saying, "With this I am shaking the foundations of the British Empire." This event sparked large-scale civil disobedience as millions of Indians began to make, buy, and sell salt illegally. A sustained movement against British colonialism succeeded in 1947, when Britain finally relented and granted India its independence.

Gandhi used self-suffering (sometimes fasting) as a way to appeal to both the British and his fellow countrymen. He commanded no army, held no government position, and was jailed or imprisoned many times, once for six years. He won Indian independence entirely through the power of disciplined nonviolence.

There are many other examples where individuals or organizations have successfully used nonviolence in confronting an oppressive force or unjust situation:

- In 1928, Abdul Ghaffar Khan converted 80,000 fierce Muslim tribesmen in the Northwest Frontier of Pakistan into the world's first unarmed, nonviolent army that liberated its people from brutal British colonial rule (evidence that Muslims can be nonviolent too).
- The Danish and other European people acted nonviolently to protect Jews from Nazi persecution in World War II.
- Lech Walesa spearheaded the nonviolent movement that led to Polish independence from Russia.
- Nelson Mandela's persistence after being jailed for twenty-six years led to a victory over apartheid in South Africa without violence.
- The Dalai Lama has stood up to the Chinese government in a long, nonviolent campaign for Tibetan freedom.

- Caesar Chavez's nonviolent movement in the 1960s and 1970s led to the protection of farmworkers' rights in California.
- And as an example of individual nonviolence and bravery, who can forget the Tank Man at Tiananmen Square, standing before a file of Chinese tanks, stopping them in their tracks?

Probably the best-known American example was the Civil Rights movement led by Dr. Martin Luther King, Jr. The 1950s and 1960s saw a campaign of boycotts, sit-ins, and marches, resulting in sweeping legislation to desegregate schools, protect voting rights, and end discrimination in housing and employment practices. Eloquently advocating nonviolence to achieve the aims of the movement, King's efforts led to the 1963 March on Washington, where he delivered his "I Have a Dream" speech. Eventually he expanded his message to address how the issues of poverty and the Vietnam War were intertwined.

Nonviolence Primer
Nonviolence is not pacifism; it is active, not passive. Pacifism believes that violence should not be resisted: turn the other cheek and hope for the best. In contrast, nonviolence wages "war" without resorting to violence. To Gandhi, inaction was the greatest sin in the face of evil or oppression. To summarize and greatly simplify, the philosophy of nonviolence is based on several main tenets.

- **Internal Nonviolence**—Nonviolence starts internally in the heart, from which external actions spring.
- **Truth Seeking**—Truth seeking means searching for the truth of a matter and clinging to that truth as you see it, neither achieving victory over another nor losing in the process. The intent is to wean the opponent from error by patience and compassion. Gandhi called this *Satyagraha.*

- **Resistance Without Violence**—Nonviolence vigorously resists someone's actions without returning the person's violence. Violence may be received but is never used against an adversary.
- **Noncooperation**—Noncooperation means refusing to participate with an oppressive, unjust, or corrupt power. This may occur through boycotts, civil disobedience, refusal to perform duties, or not accepting awards, titles, or honors. The technique is used to undermine the system's authority over the individual.
- **Relation to Rulers**—The power of an aroused populace is greater than the power of the state since government depends on the consent and the cooperation of its people. When citizens rise up, the state has a hard time stopping them.
- **No Enemies**—There are adversaries to engage, but not enemies to be defeated. One opposes the program, not the person.
- **Love Your Adversary**—Do good to those who harm you and find ways to praise those who persecute you.
- **Nonembarrassment**—Never humiliate another. It's okay to show someone that they are wrong if you show them a way out. A British politician said, "Gandhi made it impossible to govern India, but he made it possible for us to leave."
- **Law of Suffering**—You can't appeal to people with reason alone; you have to move their heart. Suffering is a remarkably effective way to do that. And if you are willing to suffer, you are demonstrating that you can't be bullied.
- **Constructive Programs**—In addition to obstructive programs that resist oppression, actions should be taken within the community to build programs and institutions that are positive alternatives to oppression.
- **Not for Sissies**—Whether nonviolent protestors face powerful fire hoses or a rabid army, nonviolence is not

for the weak of heart. Bravery surmounting that of an armed soldier is required.

- **Faith in the Future**—Nonviolence is based on the idea that the universe is on the side of justice and that peace can indeed be achieved.

One of the problems with the word "nonviolence" is that it is stated in the negative. Practitioners of nonviolence have long sought a better word. A few years ago, political scientist Dr. Glenn Paige came up with a different name with basically the same meaning but more vivid: "nonkilling." He defines a nonkilling society as a human community in which there is no killing or threats to kill, no weapons for killing, and no ideological justification for killing. This phrase (still in the negative) has several advantages:

1. "Killing" is a tangible, quantifiable word. You can count the dead bodies.
2. For those who think the word "nonviolence" is a throwback to a naive, outdated concept, nonkilling may be an easier phrase to relate to.
3. Gandhi's principles are commonly known by their Sanskrit names (nonviolent resistance = *Satyagraha*). "Killing" is a good old-fashioned English word.

Application to National Defense

In applying the concept of nonviolence to national defense, a potential deal breaker is that nonviolence and weaponry don't mix well. If you have a violent program, then tossing in some nonviolence won't help much. And in a nonviolent movement, a small amount of violence can undermine the whole program. If as a country we move toward nonviolence too quickly, we might prematurely be letting our guard down and could easily get clobbered by an enemy. So the tricky part is getting from the use of violent force to a new policy of nonviolence. In order to get there, a transition would involve a period of both nonviolence and armaments. We would have to muddle through in this imperfect situation as best we could. No one says the path to peace will be easy.

Finally, there is a **CRITICAL POINT** that needs to be made about applying nonviolence to our nation's strategic defense. Nonviolence has almost always been used by the oppressed against the oppressor. In our case, the situation is reversed: the United States, with the world's largest and most powerful weapons arsenal, is so militarily powerful that we often function in the role of the oppressor, even if we don't see it that way. There are virtually no examples where an empire has employed nonviolence as the foundation of its defense. But the objective here is not nonviolence; it's peace and national security. While the principles of nonviolence are all absolutely valid, we need to find creative ways of applying these principles as the world's sole military superpower.

> ### Story 4. Knife at the Throat
>
> If someone had a knife at your child's throat and you had a gun, would you shoot them to save your child's life? This is one of those "Gotcha" questions because if the answer is "yes," then you are not really nonviolent and if "no," then you don't care much about your child.
>
> Frankly, I don't know what I would do. First, the situation is very unlikely. Second, I don't carry a gun. Third, and this is the main point, this would be a case of personal violence, not institutional violence. They are related, no doubt. But does this situation justify war? Is it comparable to carpet bombing German cities in World War II or dropping napalm on peasants in Vietnam?
>
> Using defense of a loved one in a dark alley as a justification for war is a stretch that just doesn't work.

Peaceful Warriorship

Brief History

Most forms of martial arts are designed to do an enemy harm. However, in the 1900s, two Japanese masters diverged from this approach. Morihei Ueshiba (1883–1969) developed a form of martial arts called aikido, founded on the concept that practitioners could defend themselves while also protecting an attacker from injury.

Story 5. What about Hitler?

No discussion of nonviolence could possibly be complete without addressing the question, "What about Hitler?" Almost all will say that nonviolence could never have stopped Hitler, and if we had tried it instead of conventional warfare, we would all be speaking German today. That may be true if we had suddenly started a nonviolent movement at the beginning of World War II. But consider what might have been done prior to and during the war.

First, at the end of World War I, Europeans placed a burden of reparations and other policies on a defeated Germany that created severe economic and political stress, allowing Hitler to come into power. The economic burden placed on Germany could have been replaced with a program to rebuild the country, which might have avoided World War II just twenty-three years later.

Second, as Hitler began to consolidate his power and become a threat to the rest of the world, Germany's neighbors willingly played the role of enemy by arming to the teeth. Instead, they could have refused to enter into an arms race against him. Catholic Worker activist Karl Meyer has proposed a number of actions that European countries could have taken: a) organize a radio network around Germany to broadcast directly to the German people, refuting Hitler's distortions, b) initiate a program of free exchange vacations, inviting Germans to visit neighboring countries as guests, c) open their borders to any and all refugees from German persecution, d) announce that if Germany invaded, they would invite the soldiers into their homes and receive them as guests, not shooting at them or attempting any physical harm, and e) refuse to engage in any economic activity that would make invasion profitable.

Instead, they tried to meet German armies with deadly force, even when they were desperately outmatched, and they organized a violent underground resistance that aroused fear and anger in the invaders by assassinating German soldiers in unpredictable situations.

Third, the German people themselves might have stopped Hitler by adopting a strategy of massive, well-organized nonviolent resistance. Social Democrats and labor unions could have called for public demonstrations and a nationwide general strike involving political noncooperation by civil servants.

In fact, many ordinary people *did* apply the fundamentals of nonviolence in World War II. Outside Germany, many Jews were saved from the Holocaust by the assistance of citizens in a number of European nations, including France, Italy, Belgium, the Netherlands, Norway, Denmark, and Bulgaria.

Noncooperation included offering refuge to Jews who refused to report for deportation and organizing escape routes to transport them to safety in allied countries.

Many Germans actually thwarted Hitler's orders through noncooperation. In a display of disguised disobedience, some Nazi officials used intentional bureaucratic delays to sidetrack Hitler's orders to torture captured Allied pilots. And German scientists prevented the development of atomic weapons by deliberately arguing ad nauseam whether such weapons were feasible.

So it's not a question of whether we could have beaten Hitler with nonviolence. If nonviolent action had been taken earlier, Hitler might never have come to power, and World War II in Europe might not have happened at all.

Aikido involves the idea of harmony and balance, blending and flowing with an opponent (both literally and figuratively) to redirect the force of the attack, rather than opposing it head-on. Very little physical strength is needed, as the practitioner works with the attacker's momentum, using various throws or joint locks. While aikido styles vary in different schools around the world, most have concern for the well-being of the attacker.

Some years later, Grand Master Masaaki Hatsumi (1931–present) developed ninjutsu, a similar form of martial arts based on traditions of the ancient Japanese ninjas. The ninjas protected their villages from raiders and robbers using the arts of espionage, concealment, avoidance, and misdirection. While the early ninjas also practiced guerilla warfare, sabotage, and assassination, Hatsumi created the prototype of a new kind of warrior, dedicated to working with others without using violence. He taught how to dedicate one's life to other people and to the world as a whole. Hatsumi stated, "Ninjutsu is not only about fighting. You do it so fighting won't happen."

These forms of martial arts were introduced to the US military in 1985 when Richard Strozzi-Heckler and others conducted a top-secret experimental program called the Trojan Warrior Project. He taught awareness disciplines, including aikido and meditation, to a group of twenty-five US Army Green Berets. It must have been a challenge to teach meditation to a highly muscled man in a T-shirt reading "82nd Airborne Division, Death from Above." The program did not turn the soldiers into nonviolent warriors, but it did introduce new ideas about ethics and leadership into the Army. The results of this program are documented in the 1990 book *In Search of the Warrior Spirit*.

Further introduction of a new form of training began in 2001 with the US Marine Corps Martial Arts Program. The program trains Marines in character development in addition to physical skills. An initiator of the program was Jack Hoban, the "founding father" of ninjutsu in America, who studied for twenty-five years under Grand Master Hatsumi. Hoban gives a good explanation of the ethical training in his article "The Ethical Marine Warrior," *Marine Corps Gazette*, September 2007:

> The foundation of ethical warriorship is that "All men are created equal." Insurgents operate as if all men are *not* created equal. They don't respect the lives of those they consider nonobservant of their values. And they will kill anyone—even innocent women and children—to reach their goals.
>
> Our warrior ethics have respect for human equality as the premise—just as it is stated in our Declaration of Independence. Our warrior ethics charge us to act differently than insurgents—more respectful of all life—killing only to protect lives and when absolutely necessary. The ethical warrior shows respect for the value of life, regardless of the relative values of culture or behavior.

Hoban was mentored by the late Robert L. Humphrey, an Iwo Jima veteran and Harvard graduate, who later became a conflict resolution specialist working for the US Information Service, the Army Research Office, and the Marine Corps. He developed the Warrior's Creed, which captures the essence of the Peaceful Warrior.

Warrior's Creed

Wherever I go, everyone is a little bit safer because I am there.

Wherever I am, anyone in need has a friend.

Whenever I return home, everyone is happy I am there.

Warriorship Primer

The Peaceful Warrior, a term coined by Dan Millman in his book *Way of the Peaceful Warrior*, is an empowered and compassionate protector of others, a highly trained individual with finely tuned physical skills and a deep sense of love and reverence for life.

Peaceful Warriors may kill, but that is not their intent. In fact, the intent is just the opposite: to prevent others from killing while avoiding one's own killing, which would only occur in the most extreme of circumstances. It would never be initiated.

Peaceful Warriors find their strength and integrity by "defeating their own inner demons, living in harmony with nature, and serving their fellow man." An enemy is not seen as an abstraction to be defeated but rather as a human being with feelings, a family, and an identity. The Peaceful Warrior is slow to pick up the lance and avoids killing at almost all costs, but does not forsake killing if absolutely necessary to defend someone. While this model of warriorship involves more physical confrontation than Gandhian nonviolence, it is based on a similar respect for the humanity of an opponent.

Seeking models in both nonviolence and martial arts may sound contradictory; after all, martial arts are seen as aggressive, and nonviolence is usually viewed as passive. Actually, neither of these assertions is true. Nonviolence can be extremely aggressive, depending on how it is applied. And while enlightened martial artists are capable of barehanded lethal force, they do not use their skills to intentionally hurt others, but rather to provide loving protection for all people.

Violence and nonviolence are not opposites, like day and night. There is a spectrum of behavior from extreme violence and heavy-handed militarism at one end (Attila the Hun), to the pacifist who believes that no situation justifies killing or resistance against violence, even in defense of self and others. The three "peace churches"—Quakers, Mennonites, and Amish—generally fall into this category. Roughly in the middle lies the theory of Just War, in which war is justified if certain criteria are met

Degrees of violence and nonviolence lie within the spectrum, which can be difficult to categorize. Should the nonlethal action of throwing rocks at a tank be considered violent? What if you don't harm someone but hate the person and wish you had live ammunition; is that nonviolence? The answers lie more in one's attitudes than in actions. I argue that there is an optimal zone in which to operate somewhere in between nonviolence and Peaceful Warriorship.

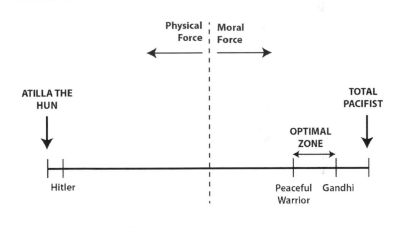

Where would you put the U.S. now?

Figure 12. Force continuum. Where would you put the United States on the force continuum today?

Application to National Defense

While the Peaceful Warriorship model applies literally to the individual, it metaphorically can be applied to national defense. If generals, military planners, and our president (who should be our ultimate Peaceful Warrior) were "armed" with this philosophy, our national defense structure would take on a completely different character. Emphasis would be placed on prevention of conflict and neutralizing an adversarial country or organization, rather than on bombing and killing as many of the enemy as possible.

It's relatively easy to imagine a martial artist defending someone without harming the attacker. It's much more difficult to extrapolate the idea to a country facing an outside threat. Nevertheless, the underlying values of Peaceful Warriorship are useful in searching for a new form of national security.

Permaculture

Brief History

After observing the destructive effects of industrial agriculture, Australians Bill Mollison and his student David Holmgren began developing ideas in the 1970s to create more sustainable agricultural systems, coining the term "permaculture" to describe their concept. While the term initially meant "permanent agriculture," its meaning quickly evolved into the notion of "permanent culture," as social aspects were seen as integral to a truly sustainable system. Mollison has described permaculture as:

> A philosophy of working with rather than against nature; of protracted and thoughtful observation rather than protracted and thoughtless labor; and of looking at plants and animals in all their functions, rather than treating any area as a single project system.

Permaculture expanded from its Australian origins to become a worldwide movement. By the mid-1980s, many students had become successful practitioners and began teaching the techniques they had learned. A global network of practicing permaculturists is now established in over one hundred countries around the world.

Permaculture Primer

Permaculture is an approach to designing agricultural systems and human settlements, modeled on the relationships found in nature.

It is based on the ecology of how things interrelate rather than on the biology of a single organism. It's a system of design where each element supports and feeds other elements to create a stable, productive system that provides for human needs and nurtures the environment. The idea of designing our lives based on natural systems is not new; our human ancestors lived this way for centuries, and indigenous cultures still do today.

In permaculture, each element is analyzed in terms of its needs, outputs, and properties. For example, the element chicken needs the elements of water and food, producing the elements meat, eggs, feathers, and manure (which can help break up the hardpan element). This synergy between design elements is achieved while minimizing waste and producing a high density of food and materials with minimal input.

Holmgren and others developed a number of key permaculture principles that guide the design of systems, including the following:

- *Use and value renewable resources and services*: reduce consumptive behavior and dependence on nonrenewable resources.
- *Integrate rather than segregate*: put the right things in the right place so that they work together to support each other.
- *Use small and slow solutions*: small and slow systems are easier to maintain than big ones and produce more sustainable outcomes.
- *Creatively use and respond to change*: carefully observe and then intervene at the right time.

While this is interesting, the part of permaculture most relevant to creating a more peaceful world is found in its set of core ethics, summarized as follows:

Earth Care: Husband the Earth. This ethic is about tending the land so it can provide for our needs, rather than function as an exploitable resource. By husbanding the Earth, we can ensure there are resources for all, develop healthy societies, and avoid harming the planet and ourselves.

People Care: Ensure that all have access to the fundamental needs of life. If we apply our creed of "Life, liberty, and the pursuit of happiness" to more than just Americans, then we have a responsibility to consider the basic needs of everyone on the planet. This ethic means that one's life is not fully complete if people on the other side of the world are suffering. This is not communism, where each gives according to their ability and each receives according to their needs. The ethic is based on the idea that our own welfare depends on the welfare of others.

Fair Share: Limit our consumption of resources and share the surplus. Reducing our consumption of energy and other resources eases pressure on the environment and increases the availability of resources to others. It also reduces the need to extract natural resources from around the world, using military force to protect that access. If we seek sufficiency rather than maximum wealth in our lives, then at the very least there is a chance that everyone can access the Earth's abundance and have their basic needs met. We can be safer and more secure if we share our surplus and contribute to a world without hunger and suffering.

Application to National Defense
Our current defense strategies are based on the opposite of permaculture ethics. Dropping defoliants on the landscape and destroying roads and bridges are not very good examples of "Earth Care." Killing civilians and calling it collateral damage isn't exactly "People Care." And invading countries to get access to their oil is a far cry from "Sharing the Surplus." Applying permaculture ethics to national defense would move us in a very different direction. Imagine what the world would be like if every politician or military general had been introduced to the concepts of permaculture in their youth.

On the face of it, the ethics of permaculture are very simple, but their implications drive deep into the heart of how we see ourselves as a people and how we view our country's role in the world. Applying permaculture ethics to our global relationships would go a long way toward creating a more just and peaceful world.

4. PEACE PRINCIPLES

**When America is no longer a threat to the world, the world
will no longer threaten us.
—Harry Browne, Libertarian**

To MOVE IN THE direction of peace, we need to fundamentally
change our national security policy. Currently, we maintain a
military presence around the globe and invade foreign countries, as
needed, to protect our perceived national interest. The new strategy
I envision is based on three Peace Principles that don't involve just
tinkering around the edges of our military system. At its core, it's
about rethinking America's role in the world and implementing
policies and programs that provide an entirely new form of national
defense. The basic idea is to base our defense on compassion rather
than on brute force, making our country secure without making
others feel insecure.

These Peace Principles apply not only to the United States but
also to any country or organization, including terrorists. Firing
rockets into Israel and using suicide bombers to strike fear into a
population are futile strategies for achieving their aims. They would
do better to rethink their mission and consider the following Peace
Principles too.

Peace Principle #1: Commit to the Well-Being of the Entire World

Why should we be committed to the well-being of the entire world? The answer is simple: because it's in our own best interest. We tend to see ourselves in competition with the rest of the world in a zero-sum game. Resources are limited, and we better get ours. What we fail to see is that when other areas of the world are suffering in deep poverty, our security is directly threatened. America's well-being depends on the well-being of every person on the planet.

Continuing to ignore the extreme poverty experienced by one third of the world's population is a dangerous mistake. As stated by Dr. John Holdren, President Obama's science advisor, "The economic and environmental predicament of the poor cannot be solved without substantial cooperation from the rich and conversely, the predicament of the poor cannot persist without peril to the rich."

Even a conservative Republican such as Senator Richard Lugar of Indiana has stated, "Eradicating global hunger must be embraced as both a humanitarian and a national security imperative."

Peace Principle #2: Protect Everyone, Even Our Adversaries

This challenging, counterintuitive concept may be the most difficult of the three principles to envision or accept. It has its foundation in the martial arts of aikido and ninjutsu, where one protects oneself and others while also protecting the attacker from injury. The practitioner works with the attacker's momentum rather than resisting the oncoming attack. If our military leaders were "armed" with this philosophy, our defensive posture would take on a completely different character. Currently, we attempt to solve a problem by defeating an enemy with our overwhelming military might. A different approach would be to neutralize, pacify, or even convert an adversary.

Peace Principle #3: Use Moral Rather Than Physical Force

Moral force means using the legitimacy of our position to undermine the political and military standing of an adversary and to rally international support for our cause. This kind of force makes the world feel less threatened and more open to peaceful resolution of conflict. It is tremendously powerful if used properly, it can be more persuasive than physical force, and it can have longer lasting, positive effects.

Physical force is a losing game. Once you start down this road, the use of force tends to escalate; it then becomes difficult to control and ultimately creates a cycle of violence. Take prisoner interrogation as an example. If some torture is good, then more torture must be better. Yet torture has very limited value at best and is the most effective tool we give terrorists to recruit new members. Ultimately, it leads toward escalation of conflict, not ending it. But mostly it undermines our own values, as we forfeit the high moral ground from which we are supposedly operating.

Story 6. A Nonviolent President?

In a sense, George Washington was our first nonviolent president. Yes, he carried a flintlock and fired at the British. But he also told his troops to behave with honor and treat captive British soldiers humanely. Washington did not seek revenge on captured British mercenaries (German Hessians) for their atrocities, which he easily could have done. Instead, his troops acted compassionately, and the captives could not believe how kindly they were treated. At one point, they were sent off marching on their own. Although they could have escaped, they all met their guards at the designated location. After the war, many of the Hessians stayed in America as settlers instead of returning home.

The message: Turn enemies into friends.

Imagine if the Peace Principles became part of our national security policy. First, we would aggressively and courageously look at how our own conduct affects people in other countries. What is the effect of our trade policies? Do American corporations have the best interests of a local population in mind when they extract the natural resources of a foreign country? What is the effect of having of our troops on foreign soil? Are there ways we can modify our behavior that would still provide for our security yet be more beneficial to the other country?

Can we provide foreign development assistance in ways that have never been tried before, benefiting the average person in the country rather than just the rich and powerful?

If, in spite of our best efforts, a threat looms, we would look for creative ways to avoid bloodshed by using diplomacy and "soft power." This does not mean diplomacy accompanied by the threat of physical force, as we do now: the carrot and stick approach. Moral force can operate on its own without military backup.

Finally, if physical action became necessary, we would use tactics with the intent of preserving life rather than taking it. Obviously, this approach allows no room for intentionally or unintentionally killing civilians.

5. PEACE PROGRAMS

Make no small plans.
—Daniel Burnham, architect

A NUMBER OF PROGRAMS are needed to implement the Peace Principles. They need to be phased in over time, and they need to work in coordination with one another; one program alone isn't sufficient to change our military posture or to convince others that we have. In developing any set of peace programs, we must remember where we are now: the world's sole military superpower with a huge arsenal of massively destructive weapons. Not only that, we have a long history of being willing to use them. With that in mind, how can we develop practical and coordinated steps to develop a new system of national defense?

The following Peace Programs are my initial cut at ideas for how we might proceed. The development of any set of programs would require a rigorous and collaborative effort on the part of many to transition to a new form of national defense.

Create a Department of Peace
Congressional proposals to create a Department of Peace began as far back as 1935. Congress came close in 1984 when it passed an act signed by President Reagan that created the US Institute of Peace (USIP). The USIP, with 325 employees working in thirty countries,

studies ways of preventing or ending violent international conflict. Its focus is on conflict prevention, conflict resolution, and postconflict stabilization, with programs to create justice systems, improve health care, build media, and expand science and technology in unstable, developing countries. While its actions are laudable, the USIP is working within our current military framework.

In 2001, Congress took its most recent step when when Dennis Kucinich (D-Ohio) introduced legislation to create a cabinet-level Department of Peace, its intent being to establish nonviolence as an organizing principle in our society. The bill has been reintroduced every year since. The current version (HR 808) is cosponsored by seventy-one members of the House of Representatives. The bill advocates peaceful, nonviolent conflict resolution at both the domestic and international levels. The responsibilities of the Department of Peace would go beyond the mandate of the USIP, with actions that include:

- training international peacekeepers;
- monitoring all domestic arms production, including weapons of mass destruction;
- promoting nonviolence in the domestic media;
- being a member of the National Security Council;
- providing advance consultation to the secretaries of state and defense prior to engagement in any armed conflict; and
- making recommendations to the president on the latest techniques for diplomacy, mediation, and conflict resolution strategies.

The basic idea is that when the president hears a proposal for military action from the Secretary of Defense, he or she can turn to the Secretary of Peace to ask, "Got any nonviolent options?" The ultimate goal of the Department of Peace would be to remove war as a necessary instrument of our foreign policy.

Conduct a Global Marshall Plan

According to the World Bank, 21 percent of the world's population lives in poverty. The UN Food and Agriculture Organization estimates that one billion people, mostly women and children, suffer from hunger and malnutrition, with a dramatic increase since 2005 due to the world economic crisis, a significant increase in food prices, and a lack of government support for agriculture relevant to the very poor. More people die from hunger and malnutrition than die from war.

Given that poverty is the greatest cause of violence, it makes sense that if people have food, shelter, and some degree of security, they are much less likely to roam the world looking to attack others. Social and military theories say that if other societies are better off, they will be less of a threat to us. So why not initiate a Global Marshall Plan (GMP), patterned after the post-WWII plan where we gave billions of dollars to rebuild the shattered economies of Europe? The program had dramatic effects, helping establish a stronger and more stable postwar world.

A modern version of the plan would go after the root causes of war and terrorism, helping needy countries move out of poverty. We would use our power, resources, and technology to design and implement a program to assist developing countries to achieve more self-sufficiency, sustainability, and improved quality of life, especially those countries that are vulnerable to takeover or could be used as a safe haven by terrorists. This kind of aid would be directed more toward the needs of the poor, such as rural transportation networks and food storage systems for small farms, rather than for huge infrastructure projects that mainly benefit the wealthy few. Support would be given in geographic areas where help is needed most, particularly in the Southern Hemisphere: southern Africa, the Middle East, Southeast Asia, and some South American countries.

Our current foreign aid program is generally not altruistic. There are exceptions, but most of our foreign aid goes to where we feel it is in our best interest: for our national security, for access to resources, or for the benefit of American corporations.

The goals of the Global Marshall Plan would instead be similar to the United Nations Millennium Development goals to assist countries in the following:

- ending poverty, hunger, and homelessness;
- developing better methods of growing, storing, and distributing food locally;
- educating children and providing adequate health care;
- dealing with the effects of climate change;
- creating sustainable economic development; and
- becoming more stable and self-sufficient.

The plan would need to be implemented by invitation only and there would be strings attached—strict transparency of government accounts and regular visits to rural areas to make sure that most of the aid breaks through the inevitable barrier of government corruption. Most critically, it must be designed to empower a country, rather than providing enabling actions that result in its dependency on outside aid. The Network of Spiritual Progressives has proposed a model Global Marshall Plan to promote this strategy. In 2008, Representative Keith Ellison (D-MN) introduced HR 1078 to promote it. Here are the main features of the plan:

- encourage all advanced industrial societies to dedicate 2 to 5 percent of their Gross Domestic Product (GDP) every year for the next twenty years to improve education and end global poverty, homelessness, hunger, and easily preventable diseases like malaria;
- create an international, nongovernmental mechanism to receive and distribute the funds; and
- create an international Peace and Justice Corps, modeled after our Peace Corps and VISTA programs, where people volunteer two years of their life to the goals of the Global Marshall Plan.

Using 2 to 5 percent of our GDP, the plan might cost the United States a few hundred billion dollars a year. While this is not a cheap proposition, it is more economical than the $1.3 trillion we annually spend on national security. The plan would be much less expensive than preparing for and conducting war, and it would provide much greater national security. Logistically, we know the plan is doable, based on our military's impressive ability to mobilize for war.

One strategy for implementing the GMP would be to target the Mideast area first in a Mideast Marshall Plan. Unemployment is very high there, it's the most volatile area of the world, and it would support the democracy movement begun in the Arab Spring of 2011.

There is a question of whether to provide aid to countries that are run by corrupt, brutal, and authoritarian regimes. Would the aid reach the needy population or support the dictatorship? This is the kind of detail that would need to be hammered out in developing the plan.

Bottom line, the idea is that global food security equals US national security. Whether the Global Marshall Plan is a naive concept or a brilliant strategy is subject to debate, but the idea has strong precedence from World War II's economic Marshall Plan. And as the world's sole superpower, we are in the best position of any country to undertake the initiative.

Create a Peace Force

We need to protect our country, but not necessarily with armed force. By transforming our armed forces into a peace force, we could provide for our national security using more peaceful means. It's not a question of eliminating the military, it's a matter of converting it.

Can people be trained to fight in a new way? If violence and killing are a basic part of human nature, so are cooperation and compassion. We have the capacity for both and the ability to choose either. If you watched the movie *Full Metal Jacket*, you have seen how effectively a tough drill sergeant can indoctrinate recruits by demeaning and dehumanizing the enemy to make killing them more acceptable. Top brass could just as easily reconstruct our existing boot camps to be Humanization Boot Camps, training young men and women to be a new kind of soldier, trained in the skills of nonviolence and Peaceful Warriorship to assist, defend, and protect people anywhere.

Soldiers want to serve, no matter how they are trained. They would respond well to being deployed for humanitarian aid in natural disasters, nonviolent peacekeeping, and other nonlethal activities. One soldier was quoted in Heckler's *In Search of the Warrior Spirit* as saying, "We just want to do something. It doesn't have to be war. We just want to put our skills to use somewhere." Rather than having an army of the meanest killers out there, we would have a highly trained, disciplined force of Peaceful Warriors with this motto: "I am a mighty warrior. I defend everyone."

The peace force would have two main functions. The first would be to implement the Global Marshall Plan. Our military has incredible technical and logistical capabilities that could be redirected. Soldiers would apply their skills in medicine, agriculture, communications, and engineering to assist people to develop self-sufficient living. Our cargo planes and aircraft carriers would provide logistical support by deploying material and personnel to needed areas. Emergency support would also be given, as we did in 2004 after the tsunami in Sumatra that killed 100,000 people and in 2010 after the earthquake in Haiti that left 1.6 million people homeless.

The second function would be to serve as an unarmed Peace Army, part of an international nonviolent peacekeeping force, physically inserting itself between warring combatants anywhere in the world. The introduction of a third party into a conflict can interrupt immediate fighting and allow time for peaceful resolution of the conflict.

There are both individual and group precedents for this effective tactic. In 1982, Mother Teresa single-handedly stopped a raging battle between Lebanon and Israel for a week so she could rescue orphans in Beirut. During the 2003 bombing of Iraq, an organization called Voices in the Wilderness took part in "human shield" actions. More than 500 foreigners positioned themselves at strategic sites such as hospitals and water purification installations to protect the local population.

There are other similar organizations: Peace Brigades International, Christian Peacemaker Teams, Witness for Peace, Volunteers for International Solidarity, Michigan Peacemaker Teams, and the Nonviolent Peaceforce (NP). Their efforts have been practiced with varying degrees of success in places like Colombia, Palestine, Sri Lanka, El Salvador, Guatemala, and the US/Mexico border.

Outside of the Department of Defense, the Central Intelligence Agency would abandon its covert operations program and return to its original mission of just gathering intelligence. There's nothing necessarily wrong with spying. It's essential to know what's going on in the world, and spying can provide information that is useful for nonviolent purposes, just as it is for military objectives.

Story 7. Nonviolent Peaceforce

The Nonviolent Peaceforce, headquartered in Brussels, Belgium, was founded by David Hartsough and Mel Duncan. During the 1984 Contra War, they observed that villages in Nicaragua were not attacked when foreigners were present, and so they started a program to train unarmed civilian peacekeepers to be deployed at a moment's notice to help solve conflicts anywhere in the world. They most often respond to invitations from local organizations committed to nonviolent solutions. Visibly nonpartisan, they arrive unarmed in NP uniforms, with NP vehicles, letting their presence be known. They meet with key players, including commanders from opposing sides; local police; and religious, business, and civil leaders in a search for peaceful resolution of a conflict.

Their activities include removing civilians from crossfire in active conflict zones and providing opposing factions a safe space to negotiate. Other activities include serving as a communications link between warring parties, securing safe temporary housing for civilians displaced by war, providing violence prevention measures during elections, and negotiating the return of kidnapped family members. Since 2002, it has been a significant force for resolving conflicts in the Sudan, the Philippines, Guatemala, and the South Caucasus countries of Armenia, Azerbaijan, and Georgia.

At least on paper, our government has taken a small step in a peace force-type direction. A November 2005 Pentagon policy statement says that making peace is a core military mission to be integrated across all Department of Defense activities, with a priority comparable to combat operations (the stick is still there). In particular, it says that we need better language skills, more regional expertise, better intelligence and counterintelligence, more emphasis on studying foreign culture, and more coordination with foreign governments and international and nongovernmental organizations. This directive is the first time that peaceful activities have been defined as a core function of the US Armed Forces.

Story 8. A New Way of Thinking?

Many in the military, especially in the officer corps, realize that our traditional military strategy left over from the Cold War is becoming increasingly outdated. They see that a new direction is needed and are supportive of change. There is a hint of this in several documents and official statements.

In 2006, General David H. Petraeus oversaw the creation of a new Counterinsurgency Field Manual, which in part states the following.

1. The more force is used, the less effective it is.
2. The best weapons for counterinsurgency do not shoot.
3. Tactical success guarantees nothing.

Nathaniel C. Flick, Center for a New American Security, edited the manual and said, "The new counterinsurgency doctrine represents a near total rethinking of the way the United States should wage war." That may be an overstatement, but it's a start. And in March 2011, Defense Secretary Robert Gates stated the following:

In my opinion, any future defense secretary who advises the president to again send a big American land army into Asia or into the Middle East or Africa should have his head examined, as General MacArthur so delicately put it.

Whether these statements represent a move away from militarism remains to be seen, but it is a hint at a possible new way of thinking by America's military.

A peace force would probably not be our first step toward demilitarization. Other programs need to be implemented first, creating less fear and resentment in the world against the United States. I envisage a gradual transition of the military toward something like a peace force, as our foreign policy and military strategy become more peacefully oriented.

End Military Invasions and Occupations

The United States is the only nation in the world able to sustain large-scale military operations over extended distances. We do so when we feel we must or when it is perceived to be in our best interest. There are many problems with using this capability.

First, this ability is tremendously expensive to maintain, and it's not just the deployment and operation cost. It's also the longer term costs of replacing damaged and lost equipment, caring for our wounded veterans, and maintaining a standby capability whether we are currently fighting or not. And after we finish a war, we often attempt to rebuild what we have destroyed in the defeated country at further cost.

Second, we may be fighting those who have a much greater stake in the conflict because they are fighting to protect their own country, or at least to maintain their power within it. In our long involvement in the Vietnam War, the Vietnamese won because they were defending their own turf from foreign invasion. The Soviets encountered a similar fate when in 1989 they gave up their war in Afghanistan, ten years after their invasion. After our ten years in Afghanistan, we are still grappling with how to "win" in a country that has been declared the "graveyard of empires."

Third, even when we think we have won, such as in the Iraq War, it is not clear what our victory has been. Terrorists are elusive, and it is difficult, if not impossible, to track them down and eliminate them, country by country. And if our stated objective is to create new democracies by an invasion, that usually hides our real interest, which may be to protect access to resources or to establish military strength in a geographically strategic location. If we really want to support the cause of democracy, it is far better that the initiative be taken through the enthusiasm and commitment of the local citizenry. We can support their cause from a distance through diplomatic and other means. A clean, nonviolent revolt of the people is much more effective in ousting a dictator than if we throw bombs into the equation.

Fourth, once we invade a country, it can be very difficult to get out. Our experience in Afghanistan is a prime example. We can't stay in it forever, and we don't know how to extract ourselves. It's like sinking in quicksand. That's because the basic premise of invading a country is flawed.

Finally, it is a fact that in every war, many more civilians are killed than soldiers. In addition, hundreds of thousands if not millions of refugees are driven from their homes, seeking safe haven. There are no smart bombs, targeted drones, or wise military strategies that can avoid this.

Should we use military force in a "humanitarian intervention" to stop genocide somewhere or to support a populist revolution in a totalitarian state? As they say in permaculture, "It depends." Doing nothing may feel morally irresponsible. But we have to look at the costs and benefits of intervention. Would our intervening make things better or worse? Can we afford to be policing the world? And if we do intervene, are we still militarily focused, sending in troops and armed drones, or do we have an unarmed peace force that can provide protection to citizens and be a third party intervener?

Close, Convert, or Donate Foreign Military Bases

Of the world's 192 countries, the United States has bases located in 135 (70 percent) of them. Many of our foreign military bases are left over from the Cold War and serve little if any use today. An oft-quoted example is our 50,000 military personnel in Germany, who are no longer needed against a nonexistent Soviet threat.

Even the Bush administration saw the wastefulness of our network of overseas bases. In 2004, then-Secretary of Defense Donald Rumsfeld announced plans to close more than one third of the nation's overseas installations, moving 70,000 troops and 100,000 family members and civilians back to the United States.

Story 9. Norway

On July 22, 2011, Anders Breivik, a right wing extremist obsessed with the "danger" of Islam, detonated a car bomb, killing eight people outside the Norwegian prime minister's office. Two hours later, he used high-powered rifles to shoot sixty-nine others at a youth camp on the island of Utoya, twenty-five miles away. As in our 9/11 attack, the people of Norway were stunned and in a state of mourning. However, unlike our response to the 9/11 attack, Prime Minister Jens Stoltenberg and the royal family all let the public see their tears on Norwegian TV; they demonstrated a determination to stand by their ideals, rather than pursuing vengeance.

Fabian Stang, the mayor of Oslo, said, "We are not going to allow fear to take hold because then we would have handed the victory to the terrorist. We are going to punish him with democracy and love."

The prime minister said, "We will meet terror and violence with even more democracy, openness, and humanity, though not without naivety." He then went on to quote a young woman who said, "If one person can show that much hate, imagine how much love we can show together."

This is very different from our response after the 9/11 attack, when we passed the Patriot Act, restricting personal freedoms in the name of security and invaded two countries, embroiling us in the last ten years of war.

National Security Adviser Jim Jones, then commander of US forces in Europe, called for closing 20 percent of our bases in Europe ("Too Many Overseas Bases," David Vine, February 25, 2009, Institute for Policy Studies). I don't know how many, if any, base closures actually occurred, but the declaration was there.

In addition to being unnecessary, overseas bases often heighten military tensions, discourage diplomatic solutions to international problems, and cause other countries to boost military spending in an escalating spiral. Overseas bases can actually make war more likely, not less. If other peace programs are implemented, the need for foreign bases will be greatly reduced if not eliminated.

Alternatively, they could be converted into "assistance centers" to benefit local populations as part of our Global Marshall Plan. The huge, permanent air bases we have opened in Iraq, for instance, could be turned educational facilities, hospitals, or any of a number of uses that would benefit the Iraqi population. In part, this would serve as reparations for the damage we have caused their country.

Phase Out Nuclear Weapons

Although the figures are elusive, the United States has about 2,300 thermonuclear (fusion) weapons in its arsenal, most on hair trigger alert (at our high point, we had 10,000 nukes out of a worldwide total of 30,000). Each warhead has tremendous explosive power, 100 to 1,000 times that of the Hiroshima (fission) bomb. The government plans to maintain this arsenal by restoring old nuclear weapons and developing a new generation of nuclear weapons in the "Reliable Replacement Warhead Program."

There are at least eight nations in today's Nuclear Club: the United States, Russia, China, France, Britain, India, Pakistan, and Israel. North Korea and Iran are the main contenders to join the list. There is also the danger of nuclear weapons reaching the hands of terrorists. Pakistani nuclear scientist A. Q. Khan has already led an illegal smuggling ring, sending nuclear components to Libya, Iran, and North Korea (he confessed but was pardoned as a national hero). Some countries such as Japan are "nuclear ready," meaning they have the material and knowledge to build a nuclear bomb within about six months.

> **Story 10. Foreign Military Base in Miami?**
>
> In 2009, the US lease on the Manta Air Base in Ecuador was set to expire. After initially refusing to renew the lease, Ecuador President Raphael Correa finally agreed, but with a caveat. He said, "We'll renew the base on one condition: that they let us put a base in Miami. If there's no problem having foreign soldiers on a country's soil, surely they'll let us have an Ecuadorean base in the US."
>
> The United States declined his proposal.

Advocates will say that nuclear deterrence has worked since the concept began after World War II. But we may have just been lucky.

The desire to eliminate the world of nuclear weapons comes from the political Right as well as the Left. President Reagan attempted, with Russian President Gorbachev, to eliminate nukes but failed to receive congressional support. In 2007, four gentlemen—

Republicans Henry Kissinger (Secretary of State under President Nixon) and George Shultz (Secretary of State under Ronald Reagan), and Democrats William J. Perry (former Secretary of Defense) and Sam Nunn (former Georgia senator)—proposed that the United States lead a worldwide program to phase out every country's nuclear weapons. Seeing this as in the national interest, their proposal included the following steps to steadily move toward a nuclear-free world:

- Extend launch decision times from the current fifteen minutes to prevent mistakes or miscalculations.
- Eliminate tactical nuclear weapons and induce Russia to do the same. Hundreds of commanders in the field agree.
- Ratify the Comprehensive Test Ban Treaty. We've signed it but not ratified it.
- Cut off production of fissile material in the world, which is capable of making 100,000 new nuclear weapons.
- Develop a consensus of all eight nuclear countries to achieve worldwide nuclear disarmament.
- Give countries fuel for nuclear reactors without letting them make bombs with it.

The last step is a tricky one. When one nation with an arsenal of nuclear weapons tells another nation it can't have even one nuke, the message is that we have the right to defend ourselves with nukes but will not allow others the same privilege. This posture can cause others to seek nuclear capability, because that seems to be the only thing we respect. To deter proliferation, the United States must take an aggressive lead in rapid nuclear disarmament. This does not mean unilateral disarmament of our nuclear capability. Rather, nuclear weapons need to be phased out in coordination with the other nuclear powers. Recent initiatives by President Obama and Russian President Medvedev to reduce the arsenal of American and Russian nukes are a step in the right direction.

Stop Arming the World

In 2010, global spending on arms and military technology was an estimated $1.6 trillion, with nearly half of the sales by the United States. The largest arms sale in history occurred that year in the volatile Middle East, when we sold $123 billion worth of arms to Saudi Arabia, the United Arab Emirates, Kuwait, and Oman (*Financial Times*, September 2010). Arms sales cover the gamut, including tear gas, armored vehicles, shoulder-fired missiles, surface-to-air missiles, and aircraft carriers. Weapons makers are well subsidized by Washington through tax breaks, funds for marketing, and default protection for loans made to arms buyers. Sales of arms abroad are used to fortify our allies, even dictatorships, and to maintain a balance of power, as when we sold arms to both Iran and Iraq prior to the Gulf War.

The leading defense contractors—Lockheed Martin, Boeing, Northrup Grumman, General Dynamics, and Raytheon—depend on arms sales for a significant portion of their revenue. While arms sales are very profitable, they can be counterproductive to national security. Lawrence Korb, a former Reagan Department of Defense official, says, "It has become an absurd spiral in which we export arms, only to have to develop more sophisticated ones to counter those we already spread all over the world."

Where American-sold weapons end up is a crapshoot. Some of the weapons we provided the Mujahedeen to fight the Soviet Union in Afghanistan ended up in the hands of al Qaeda. In 2009 and 2010, we sold Libya $63 million in arms that could have been used against us when we attacked Libya in 2011. And at that time, we were in the middle of negotiating another $77 million arms deal with Muammar Kaddafi.

We may have only limited control to stop nuclear proliferation. But it is entirely within our control to stop arming the countries of the world and to encourage them to move toward demilitarization as we demilitarize here at home.

Reduce Defense Spending

If you think that government is too big and that our federal budget is obscenely bloated, remember that our national security budget consumes 62 percent of total federal discretionary spending. If you want to cut your household budget, you start with where you spend most—the highest cost item. Let's consider that idea for our federal budget.

Scaling back our national security spending to half its current level would reduce the current cost from $1.3 trillion to $650 billion. Could we still be safe at this level? We would still be outspending every other country by far. What kind of military advantage do we need over everyone else? Which obsolete weapon systems would we eliminate? Which military programs are not critical? What are the core programs that we would have to retain to maintain our security (intelligence gathering, for example, that would allow us to see problems far enough in advance to develop nonviolent solutions)? Would the cuts be more feasible if we implemented the proposed Peace Programs?

Reduced defense spending is not so much a proposal as a promise. The American economy cannot sustain its current level of deficits and national debt, so we won't be able to maintain military operations as we have in the past. So far, the military budget has been sacrosanct—no politician has been willing to touch it. But the elephant in the room is being discovered, and cutting the defense budget should appeal to both fiscal conservatives and antiwar liberals. Given that Americans have an intolerance of high taxes, inefficient government, and anything negatively affecting their pocketbook, citizen pressure may soon push politicians to significantly trim defense spending.

If, in fact, the annual $1.3 trillion for national security were reallocated, one third could remain for national security, one third could go toward infrastructure building/social programs, and one third toward reducing the federal debt. Without even closing loopholes for corporations and the wealthy, or otherwise increasing taxes, $433 billion could be available annually for national security (still five times the defense spending of China, which has the world's second largest defense budget), $433 billion for infrastructure to create jobs here at home, and $433 billion to reduce the national debt. Over ten years, that would represent 30 percent of our current national debt.

Convert the Defense Industry

Conversion of the defense industry to civilian production has been studied in think tanks since the end of the Cold War. Defense contractors make up a significant portion of our economy. If we stopped producing weaponry and fighting wars, that would throw millions of Americans out of jobs and create havoc with investors' portfolios. Fortunately, there are two viable methods that could save the industry and jobs.

The first is called "steering the work." When Boeing and Lockheed were competing for a very large aviation contract, the federal government preferred Lockheed's design but gave the contract to Boeing to bolster Seattle's sagging economy (and then they required Boeing to use Lockheed's design!). The point is that the government can compensate for the loss of defense jobs by steering other work to former defense contractors. Defense plants could be retooled for programs such as innovative low cost housing, more effective global food distribution systems, and cheap electric cars with a 500-mile range.

An example of a straightforward conversion would be for a company that builds destroyers to make hospital ships instead for humanitarian relief programs. We accomplished a massive conversion from peacetime to wartime production in World War II, and we can do it again, just in the opposite direction.

The second remedy has strong roots in national policy: the concept of subsidies. If the government can provide subsidies to dairy farms and the nuclear power industry or bailouts to failing investment banks because it's in the national interest, it can support a defense industry in transition. The objective is not to dismantle the defense industry but to convert it.

Even without government assistance, the defense industry may find a way through a transition. If they see that wars are diminishing, the demand for weapon systems is drying up, and their lobbying is failing, they will most likely look for alternative ways to make a

Story 11. Costa Rica

There are approximately twenty-five countries in the world that have no armed forces. After a bloody civil war in 1949, Costa Rica constitutionally abolished its military forces, the first country to demilitarize in the twentieth century. Since then, its history has been peaceful and it has had a rising standard of living, earning the nickname "Switzerland of the Americas." The country has universal health care and education, operates with 95 percent renewable energy sources, has restored its rainforest, is considered "business friendly," and comes closest of any country to the sustainability concept of "one planet living."

Costa Rica is not a perfect country. But it demonstrates what can happen when a military force is eliminated and resources are rechanneled in other directions.

profit. While having to change a corporate culture, retool, and go into a new line of work may not be a chief executive's dream, it beats going out of business.

An ancillary benefit of defense conversion would be increased jobs in the American economy. A 2007 study at the University of Massachusetts, Amherst, determined that for every $1 billion spent in the military, more than twice as many jobs would be created in the civilian sector for the same amount of money.

Right now, our economy needs war to function. Conversion of the defense industry is a way to thrive economically without war.

PART III

How to Get There

6. FORCES FOR CHANGE

The people must lead so the leaders can follow.
—Mahatma Gandhi

How will the change to a more peaceful society come about? Ralph Nader in his novel *Only the Rich Can Save Us!* proposed that a movement of liberal billionaires led by Warren Buffett can return the country back to the people. Maybe. Or change might come from an enlightened political leader, a President Gandhi, but it's not a good bet. Corporate and military power are so deeply rooted in our political system that such a leader could not be elected; even if elected, he or she would not be able to buck the system. While the best case is for change to come simultaneously from the top down and the bottom up, the force for change is much more likely to come from the bottom, as citizens initiate, promote, and demand the change.

Citizen Action
The power of individuals to collectively bring about social change is huge. In his book *Blessed Unrest,* Paul Hawken describes a nonideological movement under way in the world that mostly flies under the radar of the media. It is a powerful, nonviolent, grassroots movement that has no cluster bombs, no armies, and no drones. The participants come from different cultures and a range

of social classes. At least one million organizations in the world are working toward peace, social justice, and environmental protection, probably many more. The *New York Times* has called it the Second Superpower. What's lacking is a coordinated merging of the different groups to become a major political force, as has happened with the Tea Party.

But how big a difference can one person or organization make politically compared to the power of a defense contractor that receives $15 billion worth of weapons contracts a year, makes huge political contributions, and aggressively lobbies Congress around the clock? Even a president who believes in peace has his or her hands tied, given the enormous power of the economic and political elite.

It sounds daunting, but never underestimate the power of a social movement whose time has come. While our politicians may seem to be marching to their own tune, remember that we, the people, elect them. And consumers, accounting for 70 percent of GDP, have tremendous economic and political leverage when used collectively.

As the political Left and Right battle it out on the airwaves, people on both sides of the spectrum are finding common ground. On the right, even conservative Glenn Beck stated in April 2010, "Cut the military budget in half and bring our troops home." And Defense Secretary Robert Gates has said something that sounds like a Global Marshall Plan: "There is need for a dramatic increase in spending on the civilian instruments of national security: diplomacy, strategic communications, foreign assistance, civic action, and economic reconstruction and development."

One individual has already created a kind of mini Global Marshall Plan. In spite of his current bad press, Greg Mortenson, the author of *Three Cups of Tea* and *Stones into Schools*, single-handedly raised money to build hundreds of schools for children, mostly girls, in Pakistan and Afghanistan. By educating girls, the intended effects are to lower birthrates and infant-mortality rates, improve the quality of village life, and reduce the recruiting of terrorists through the empowerment of women ("Forget joining that jihad group, my son.").

Citizen action appears to have recently reached a major breakthrough. On September 17, 2011, a few thousand people gathered in the financial district of New York City answering the call of *Adbusters* magazine for a peaceful occupation of Wall Street to protest a rigged economic and political system. At the end of the day, about two hundred people set up camp in Zuccotti Park and started what became a national—and now international—movement.

At the time of this writing, the Occupy Wall Street movement (We are the 99%) has spread to hundreds of other cities around the United States and worldwide to over 1,500 cities involving hundreds of thousands of people. The protesters include the long-term unemployed, the Millennials who are entering the worst job market in recent history, victims of bank foreclosures, public employees facing budget cuts, and veterans returning from Iraq and Afghanistan who can't find work. Many people who never previously carried a protest sign were inspired to join the movement.

Inspired by the Arab Spring and uprisings in Europe, it is decentralized with no single leader. Decision-making is based on consensus in daily meetings called General Assemblies.

While criticized for not having a clear, coherent set of demands, the movement is basically stating one thing: that our political and economic systems are broken and the status quo cannot continue. The Occupy movement, as it has come to be called, seeks deep changes in our society, not temporary fixes or single-issue reforms.

How successful this movement will be remains to be seen, but it is this kind of citizen uprising that will be required to bring about a change in Washington. The Occupy movement has already altered the national conversation to focus on the needs of the average American, rather on the wealthy few. In the words of Sarah van Gelder, author of *This Changes Everything*, "Historians may look back at September 2011 as the time when the 99 percent awoke, named our crisis, and faced the reality that none of our leaders are going to solve it. This is the moment when we realized we would have to act for ourselves."

New Business Models

Poverty is one of the root causes of violence and war. If the empowerment of people results in less poverty and more economic equality, then businesses that accomplish this end are making a contribution to peace. New business models are emerging that represent creative ways to empower people as a core part of their mission.

Microcredit

In 1976, Bangladeshi economics professor Muhammad Yunus loaned $26 to forty-two Bangladeshi villagers. That was the start of Grameen Bank, dedicated to improving the lives of millions of poor, particularly in rural areas of underdeveloped countries. This "bank for poor people" makes small loans, as small as $5 to $25, to help people set up micro-businesses. The many branches of the bank are self-funded by their depositors, who become owner-members. Profits are redistributed to the owner-members or are invested in community projects. The system keeps the money, including interest payments, continuously circulating to build local community wealth.

As of 2010, the bank has lent $9 billion; 97 percent of these loans are to women. Through the small businesses started with these loans, more than one third of Grameen's clients have now been raised out of poverty. Other microcredit programs replicating the Grameen model have spread across the world.

Social Entrepreneurs

Some entrepreneurs are creating businesses for the purpose of aiding others, not for their own financial gain. One example is Iqbal Quadir, a Bangladeshi who moved to the United States and became a New York investment banker. He later developed the idea to get cell phones into the hands of the poor in rural areas of his home country. In 1993, he founded Gonofone (Bengali for "phones for the masses"), which later became GrameenPhone.

Seeing the telephone as a weapon against poverty, Quadir's vision was to create universal access to telephone service in Bangladesh to increase self-employment opportunities for its rural poor. Working with Grameen Bank, GrameenPhone lends money to village women to buy cellular telephones. They in turn sell time on the phone to fellow villagers, which generates income for the women to pay off their loans. Villagers then use the telephones to reach suppliers and customers, generating their own additional income.

Today, GrameenPhone provides cellular coverage to more than 100 million rural people living in 60,000 villages throughout Bangladesh; it has expanded to provide services to other countries and generates revenues close to $1 billion annually. Quadir's success has been lauded as a model of bottom up development, improving economic opportunity and empowering citizens in poor countries around the world.

Cooperatives

The standard American company has owners and workers; these groups tend to be in opposition to each other. An innate tension results as owners and managers want to maximize profits and workers want to maximize their compensation. This is an unnecessary dichotomy. An alternative business model is cooperatives, where workers own and manage their own business, which can be considered a third form of business compared to socialism or capitalism.

In 1974, the United States created one version of this concept in an Employee Share Ownership Plan (ESOP), where a corporation gives staff members shares in the company as part of their compensation. ESOPs are most commonly used to motivate and reward employees and to provide a market for the shares of departing owners. ESOPs are not the same as cooperatives, as ESOP employees do not have an equal vote in managing the company. The management/worker polarity still exists. Cooperatives, in contrast, provide both ownership and a direct voice in company management.

There are many cooperatives in existence today, the largest being a federation of worker-owned cooperatives called the Mondragon Corporation, based in the Basque region of Spain. Founded in 1956, it has become a $15 billion entity, employing 85,000 people working in 256 businesses. It has its own bank, a university of 8,500 students, and a Peace Center that trains people in ethics and conflict resolution.

Their worker-members own the cooperatives, and power is based on the principle of one person, one vote. Workers elect their management, receive a living wage, and share in the profits, which are divided among all the workers. The wage ratio between the worker-owners who do executive work and those who work in the field or factory averages 6:1, in contrast to the average ratio of 400:1 or more for US CEOs. The CEO of the entire Mondragon Corporation earns only nine times as much as the lowest paid worker in the entire complex.

The businesses operate in the areas of banking and insurance, manufacturing of consumer goods and industrial components, retail sales, and construction. Among other things, Mondragon is an integral supplier for the world's leading car manufacturers. Since its founding, Mondragon has expanded its operations to eighteen countries around the world, including Brazil, China, France, Germany, and India. In October 2009, the United Steelworkers announced an agreement with Mondragon to create worker cooperatives in the United States.

Socially Responsible Capitalism

Capitalism is based on the ideas that we can do anything we can imagine and everyone has a chance to get ahead. But capitalism can take different forms. Our Western style of capitalism is based on growth and maximizing profits regardless of the effect on people and the planet. It is founded on the principle of the common good resulting from the private pursuit of profit. One can argue whether our regulations are too strict or too lax, but some government regulation is required to maintain a relatively level playing field. But when government is too weak or corrupt to properly regulate, the environment suffers unnecessarily, wealth inequality increases, and the system no longer functions well.

A different form of capitalism is emerging with a triple bottom line: people, planet, and profit. This means that a company's social and ecological performance is taken into account, along with financial performance, in measuring success. These firms receive a satisfactory return on investment, have decent CEO salaries, take care of their workers, and operate as good corporate citizens. The welfare of employees is given a high priority, and the company uses sustainable environmental practices. The company's responsibility lies more with stakeholders (i.e., those who are influenced directly or indirectly by the actions of the firm), rather than just with the shareholders who own the company. These are some companies that follow this principle:

- Whole Foods, which has proven that selling organic foods can be profitable;
- Novo Nordisk, a Danish pharmaceutical company dedicated to ridding the world of diabetes;
- GrupoNueva of Chile, having a goal of creating a sustainable Latin America;
- Grameen Danone Foods, a joint venture between a $16 billion multinational yogurt maker and the Grameen microcredit bank; and
- Seventh Generation, the nation's leader in green detergents and related products, whose policy is that no one be paid more than fourteen times the lowest base pay.

Certain states have passed laws allowing companies to register as B Corporations ("B" stands for "benefit"), which allows a company to subordinate profits to social and environmental goals so that a CEO can't be sued by shareholders for not making profit the sole obligation. Four states—Vermont, Maryland, New Jersey, and Virginia—have passed B legislation, with many others expected to follow.

Creating a socially responsible business is voluntary, not government mandated, which should appeal to conservatives. American capitalism is extremely flexible, and a company can change on a dime when it wants to or when it has to. Over time, it can adapt as necessary to a changing world and an evolving social consciousness.

Localization
The idea of economic localization is the polar opposite of the globalization of international trade. Prior to globalization, economies

were much more localized within a community or within a country. Now products are manufactured on one side of the world and shipped to the other. While globalization has its benefits, opposition to it was dramatized by the 1999 Seattle demonstrations against the World Trade Organization. There are many downsides to globalization that effect prospects for peace, including:

- an explosion of freight traffic that increases fossil fuel consumption, fuel prices, and levels of carbon emissions;
- long supply chains and just-in-time inventory strategies, causing vulnerability to interruption from catastrophes such as the 2011 Fukushima nuclear disaster in Japan;
- companies that relocate to countries with the weakest environmental and labor laws;
- a growing flow of immigrants across borders;
- potential loss of traditions and cultures in an interconnected world;
- a growing gap between rich and poor, as the disadvantaged in society are left behind by globalization;
- the movement of real power from citizen democracies to global corporations; and
- concentrated control of the world's food supply.

The Transition movement, begun in Great Britain in 2005, represents an alternative to globalization. Transition Towns are communities that reorganize locally in response to the twin problems of peak oil and climate change to become more self-reliant and resilient to shocks coming from the outside. The movement largely bypasses the "system" and prepares for the possible breakdown of the mainstream economy.

The key features of the movement are described by Rob Hopkins in *The Transition Handbook* as 1) a shift to a lower-energy, more localized social structure, 2) having locally produced food, energy, waste management, currency, governance, and culture, and 3) living more within our means, creating a simple, full life. Localization includes the following actions:

- producing, shopping, and employing locally;
- using barter, local currency, local banks, and a credit and lending system much like the savings and loans associations we had before the 1970s;
- reducing consumption with the idea that if communities are strong enough for one to count on, individual accumulation of wealth is less important;
- developing sustainably so that the needs of the present can be met without compromising the ability of future generations to meet their own needs (the seventh generation principle); and

Story 12. Argentina
From the documentary *Argentina: Turning Around* by Melissa Young and Mark Dworkin

You don't need a Transition Town movement to accomplish change—circumstances can force it on you, as happened in Argentina.

In the 1990s, the government of Argentina pursued an economic strategy of globalization, deregulation, and privatization. The result was the 2001 collapse of the economy, business failures, soaring unemployment, and a paralyzed government. Existing institutions were no longer responding to people's needs for jobs, education, and health care.

Spontaneously, the people of Argentina took matters into their own hands. They took over unused banks, created large-scale community gardens, and blockaded streets and highways daily to demand government action. Hundreds of factories that had been abandoned by the owners were reopened in defiance of the law. Workers went into business for themselves, creating worker-owned cooperatives. Committees ran the new businesses, and income was divided equally among each group. Without managerial experience, they figured out how to run things as they went along.

The Argentinian economy recovered substantially from 2004 to 2007 and pulled through the global depression of 2007–2010 well, as unemployment dropped from 25 to 8 percent, its entire debt to the IMF was paid off, and growth reached a high of 9 percent in 2010.

- pushing primary government down to the level of local councils and communities. This is consistent with the conservative view that government should be brought down to the lowest possible level.

The aim of the Transition movement is a graceful and elegant descent from our overconsumptive society by beginning now to make necessary changes. If the Transition Town principles are broadly applied, the result would be a significant reduction in consumption of natural resources, reducing the pressure for war and buying the world more time to deal with the growing problems of population, climate change, and energy. Since its beginning, the movement has spread to over 340 officially designated Transition Towns around the world.

Interestingly, Transition Towns are based on the same principles as Gandhi's concepts of self-government (*Swaraj*) involving small-scale, decentralized government and local economy (*Swadeshi*), where whatever is produced locally is used foremost by the members of that community. He believed that a community should be independent of its neighbors for its own vital wants and yet interdependent for needs where dependence is a necessity.

Role of Gender
Women are the peacemakers of the world. Whether this generalization is due to genetic or cultural reasons, research shows that there is a strong correlation between the empowerment of women and a reduced tendency of a nation to engage in armed conflict:

> As women are empowered socially and economically, and as they take their rightful place in the councils of government, the tendency to resort to violence and use force as a means of settling difference diminishes.... In most cases, when women gain positions of power, greater emphasis is placed on the nurturing aspects of society and less on the militaristic ones. Police and defense budgets decrease and so do violence and crime

rates. ("Gender Empowerment and the Willingness of States to Use Force": paper presented by Monty and Donna Ramsey Marshall, International Studies Association, February 19, 1999).

Story 13. Nobel Women

In 1901, Norwegian Alfred Nobel created the Nobel Peace Prize to honor "the person who has done the best work for fraternity between nations, the abolition or reduction of standing armies, and the holding and promotion of peace conferences." Since that time, fifteen women have received the prize:

1905: **Baroness Bertha von Suttner**, an Austrian peace activist and author
1931: **Jane Addams**, an American peace advocate active in the effort to forge an end to World War I
1946: **Emily Green Balch**, an American academic who campaigned against entry into World War I
1977: **Betty Williams**, an advocate of nonviolence from Northern Ireland, and **Mairead Corrigan**, an activist who worked with Williams to end the fighting in Northern Ireland
1979: **Mother Teresa**, a Roman Catholic nun, who aided the "poorest of the poor"
1982: **Alva Myrdal**, a Swedish social scientist who was a strong advocate for disarmament
1991: **Aung Sang Suu Kyi**, a nonviolent activist for human rights in Myanmar (Burma)
1992: **Rigoberta Menchu Tum**, a nonviolent activist for indigenous rights in Guatemala
1997: **Jody Williams**, an activist who led the International Campaign to Ban Landmines
2003: **Shirin Ebadi**, an attorney who campaigned for the rights of women and children in Iran
2004: **Wangari Maathai**, the late Kenyan activist who founded the Green Belt Movement
2011: **Ellen Johnson Sirleaf**, first elected president of Liberia, **Leymah Gbowee**, Liberian peace activist, and **Tawakkul Karman**, Yemeni journalist and women's rights activist

Social scientist Dr. Riane Eisler, in her book *The Real Wealth of Nations,* concludes the following:

> Abandoning our preoccupation with material wealth and profits and elevating ourselves to a more empathetic worldview will require embracing feminine characteristics that foster peaceful communities and sustainable economies. More of our cultural icons in the future will be women and also men who reflect the nurturing aspects of leadership.

There are many women's peace organizations around the world, including Women for Peace, the Women Waging Peace Network, Code Pink, Peace x Peace, and the Women's International League for Peace and Freedom. If American women move to the forefront of social change, we should see a "gentling" of our foreign and military policies. Some men may fear a rise of women to higher positions in politics or dread a feminization of our foreign policy. But men can learn a lot from women and still be men.

7. TIMING OF CHANGE

Nothing endures but change.
—Heraclitus, Greek philosopher

IT WILL TAKE SOME time to shift from a culture of war to a culture of peace, but how long? On the one hand, mankind has used violent means to solve our problems for millennia. It's unlikely that we can adopt a new approach overnight. On the other hand, our world is changing very rapidly, and we appear to be in the beginning of a transformational time. Perhaps we can reach a more peaceful world within a generation.

Phases of Change
Whatever the time frame, change will probably occur in a series of phases as illustrated in Figure 13.

Phase 1: Awareness Raising
In Phase 1, the public recognizes that there is a problem, and citizen movements put pressure on government and businesses to reform. The media, with a growing understanding that change is in the wind, start reporting on the movement, and a few politicians get elected who reflect the new point of view. One element at a time, the transition builds. Along the way, there are successes and setbacks, as

the entrenched use their mighty strength to fight against the forces of change.

Do we strip ourselves of all our weapons in this phase? I would argue "No," because the foundation for change must be laid first. It takes time to adopt and implement policies that reduce our need for weaponry. While this may not be a purist approach, I think it is a realistic and feasible one. As we change our mind-set, adjust our military posture, and experience success with a more charitable and inclusive approach to international relations, we can begin to wean ourselves from the weapons of war. The intent is that eventually we would have enough confidence in both ourselves and in a new world order to beat the last sword into a plowshare.

Phase 2: Transition

IN PHASE 2, SOME kind of transformational event occurs—the bursting of a huge economic bubble, some dramatic catastrophe caused by a military miscalculation, or a sudden spike in the price of gasoline to an unimaginable level. I don't know how bad the event will be, but I do believe it will be enough to change life as we know it. Whatever it is, the event could provide the leverage point needed for a major change in our society.

However it occurs, the walls will crumble, and even the greatest skeptics will see that old policies must be changed. A champion will emerge in the form of an individual or organization that gains popular support and goes on the offensive to develop and implement new policies.

Hopefully, we can take actions before a crisis point is reached, but that's not how humans seem to operate. We need a big crisis crashing down before we are willing to give up comfortable positions and unsustainable habits.

In Phase 2, the Pentagon would be rethinking its military strategy, given its much lower operating budget and a declining supply of fuels. In foreign affairs, the dominant role would shift from the Defense Department toward the State Department, with greater emphasis placed on cooperative diplomacy than on armed force.

The transition would involve what economists call dislocations. Just as modern technology displaces people working in older technologies, there would be a period of adjustment. Defense contractors would be shifting to new areas of research, development, and production. Revenues, profits, and jobs in major corporations would still be there, though the numbers may not be as high. People will be working on more productive and socially beneficial projects in this transitional phase.

Phase 3: Institutionalization

Finally, in the third phase, new policies and programs become institutionalized as the norm. The US economy is no longer dominated by a huge military system, and a peace economy emerges. We will have adopted true compassion (not the type know as "compassionate conservativism") as the basis for our domestic programs and foreign policy. As a result, fear and hatred of America will diminish around the world, and we will observe a rapidly dwindling terrorist threat. Our country regains its stature as an admired and respected nation.

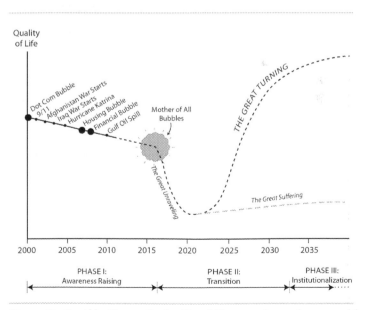

Figure 13. Possible Change Paths. The shift to a culture of peace could occur in a series of phases.

Possible Change Paths

While we don't know exactly what the future will be, we can hypothesize what a change path might look like.

The first decade of this century saw a series of events causing a steady decline in what I'll call the quality of life for most Americans: 9/11 and wars in Afghanistan and Iraq; the dot.com, housing, and financial bubbles; a severe recession; an unprecedented hurricane that demolished New Orleans; and the Gulf Coast oil spill, the largest in our history.

Sometime in this second decade (very likely before 2015), we may hit that Mother of All Bubbles that causes the end of life as we have known it. Things will almost certainly get worse, perhaps much worse, and there will be great confusion and much suffering, what economist Paul Krugman has called the Great Unraveling. There may be institutional collapse, global depression, mass human migrations, and widespread starvation. I hate to paint too horrible a picture, but it could be that bad. However, this would also be the teachable moment, when it is clear that our traditional assumptions are obsolete and the time is right for a new message to be heard. The question is, where do things go from there?

The Great Turning

At this point, things are likely to go in one of two ways. The pessimistic view is that we enter a period that can be called the Great Suffering, where world society as we know it collapses; governments worldwide become authoritarian; and the rich elite live in guarded, gated communities while the poor majority are figuratively (and perhaps literally) locked outside. Survivalists hole up in the mountains with food stashes and their rifles locked and loaded. It could be something as dismal as the Dark Ages of the fifth to twelfth centuries.

The more optimistic view is that we will experience what scholars Dr. David Korten and Dr. Joanna Macy have called the Great Turning: a time of extraordinary reinvention and rebuilding of our world. They see this as the third in a series of great revolutions in the history of mankind. The Agricultural Revolution began about 10,000 BC and lasted centuries. The Industrial Revolution that moved us into the modern age started just two hundred years ago. The third revolution, the Great Turning, will be a transformational moment similar in scope and magnitude to the two previous revolutions, just needing to happen much faster and much more thoroughly.

The Great Turning from an industrial growth society to a "life-sustaining society" has three components that are mutually supportive.

1. Activism—People engage in the holding actions needed to slow down the worst of the damage: protest marches, soup kitchens, legal challenges.
2. Structural Change—New institutions begin to replace the old, including new ways of growing food, new forms of education, new measures of prosperity, and a new military structure.
3. Shift in Consciousness—People develop a new spirituality based on ancient wisdom traditions, which believe that we are all connected to each other and are one with the Earth.

In a groping way, society would search for a new way of organizing. Initially, the turning might be based on economics, as people are forced into far less consumptive lifestyles. A culture of rugged individualism would shift toward a model of cooperation as people rely more on their neighbors and local community for support. As people discover that their new lifestyle is actually more satisfying, they will experience a kind of spiritual reawakening.

Crime surprisingly abates and the prison population declines as restorative justice replaces the current punitive criminal system. The global economy is forced to compete with strong new local economies. The American economy becomes centered more on Main Street than Wall Street. GDP is replaced by an economic measure that's more like Bhutan's Gross National Happiness (GNH) model (see Story 15). National security shifts away from militarism as defense budgets are drastically cut. Foreign military bases are sequentially closed. We replace threat and force with a spirit of compassion as the basis of our foreign and national security policies. It would be a rite of passage to a new culture of global peace, ecological sustainability, social justice, and spiritual fulfillment: a postcarbon society.

Will we go the route of the Great Suffering or the Great Turning? It's up to us. In the words of Joanna Macy, "We're not sure how the story will end. It's that knife's edge of uncertainty where we come alive and feel our greatest power."

Rate of Change
The Great Turning may sound too good to be true. But rapid, largely unanticipated change has happened many times before:

1776	The American Revolution, which defeated a much stronger British army
1865	Abolition of slavery in the United States after 200 years
1920	Women's right to vote, denied for 140 years
1941	The incredible US industrial ramp up at the beginning of World War II
1960s	The Civil Rights movement that overturned segregation
1969	Man's first walk on the moon
1993	Creation of the European Union after countries had fought each other for centuries
1994	The end of apartheid in South Africa
2008	Election of the first African-American president
2011	The Mideast uprising for democracy

Given the rate at which change is accelerating in the world, a change toward peace could come very rapidly, perhaps in one generation. If a generation is defined as twenty years, then we're talking about the year 2031. How old will you be then? Can you imagine a transition to peace happening that fast?

Obstacles to Overcome
This topic should be the book's longest section, given the large number of obstacles in the way of peace. Some of these obstacles may be obvious, but it's worth reminding ourselves of them. Let's start with belief systems.

Story 14. Future Worlds
From "On the Very Real Possibility of Transformational Change"
by Marjorie Kelley of the Tellus Institute, a Boston think tank

This article is one of the best-written, most succinct descriptions I have read of where we are and where we may be headed. Here it is, condensed.

1. Where we are now: global warming, end of the petroleum age, growing wealth inequalities around the world.

2. Future population growth from 7 billion to 9 billion by 2050. This and other factors cause things to get worse before they have a chance to get better.

3. There are four possible futures.

A. **Market Forces Scenario**—Business continues as usual. The current rate of resource consumption continues, and other nations tend toward American lifestyles. The result is rising sea levels, unprecedented species extinction, pains of withdrawal from fossil fuels, greater frequency of droughts and hurricanes, and prolonged economic downturn.

B. **Policy Reform Scenario**—Government embraces ambitious policies to reduce energy use, carbon emissions, hunger, and economic inequality. The changes come too little and too late—social and ecological systems collapse.

C. **Fortress World Scenario**—Reforms fail and problems cascade. The affluent live in protected enclaves amid oceans of misery. Governments focus on security and employ draconian control measures. The world order collapses into a group of police states.

D. **Great Transition Scenario**—Higher fuel prices and carbon constraints prod us to embrace traveling less, consuming less, and living in smaller houses in more self-sufficient communities. There is not a sense of deprivation because people recognize that quality of life matters more than quantity of stuff. Conspicuous consumption is seen as a vulgar throwback to a coarser time. We see the need to guarantee a decent minimum wage for everyone on the planet, as the factors driving war fade away. Transformation would be an achievement against all the odds, just as we previously faced insurmountable odds like in the American Revolution, where a tiny, ragtag band of revolutionaries took on the most powerful empire on the planet, and won.

In the long run, the choice is between the scenarios C and D: unstable fascism or a positively transformed world. Tipping points can pitch us into either. What unlocks positive social transformation is a shift in values. Our challenge is to face our own entrenched habits and reconceptualize our place in the world. Liberals will have as hard a time making the change as conservatives.

Belief Systems

Many believe humanity's highest achievements are reached in the courage and honor of war. If you believe in a "just war" and believe that things are more or less fine as they are, then peace may be impossible to even envision. But today, many things are challenging our traditional beliefs. For cynics, the Peace Principles and Peace Programs may seem naive and unrealistic, but so is the idea that war can bring peace. All of the world's revolutionary ideas have at first been ignored, then ridiculed, eventually tolerated, and finally seen as self-evident. Accepting the ideas outlined here may be no different.

Entrenched Powers

Those in power or on the receiving end of half of the federal budget have a lot invested in the way things are. Wars often improve a president's popularity and always deliver profits to industry. And the absence of war means giving up our cherished role as a military superpower. You may say the elite would never abandon militarism. But if the American people demand peace, they can overcome the resistance of the entrenched.

Allure of Violence

Our weapons are extremely powerful and crank up a man's testosterone. Think of the young soldier who rolls over houses in an armored tank that puts his SUV back home to shame. What's needed is excitement redefined. War can be exhilarating as we struggle against the forces of evil. With Peaceful Warriors, protecting people can be just as satisfying, like what firefighters experience when pulling someone out of a burning building.

Nationalism

Commitment to the nation-state is probably something that will never go away, and perhaps it shouldn't. But defining patriotism as "my country no matter what" stifles critical thinking and muffles the dissent that our country was founded on. Devotion to the well-being of one's country is a good thing, unless it excludes the well-being of all others on the planet.

Nationalism needs a new definition, something involving a belief in the equality of all people and a commitment to international cooperation.

Inertia

At both the personal and governmental level, inertia is tough to overcome. It's so easy to continue what we've always done. And it's hard to prevent war when a society is perpetually armed and prepared for it. We are comfortable with military defense. As a friend of mine said, "I like being defended." It will probably take a major shock, a rude awakening of some kind, to escape the inertia.

Fear

We fear change because it threatens our comfort zone. Letting go of our safety shield—our soldiers and our high tech weapons—is a frightening idea that may feel like we're going naked in the world.

Nevertheless, there have been politicians and world leaders who have overcome their fears or prejudices to reach beyond prior positions. Egypt's Anwar Sadat, who led the 1973 Yom Kippur War against Israel, later went to speak for peace in the Israeli Knesset. Alabama Governor George Wallace, best known for his belligerent defense of segregation in the turbulent 1960s, mellowed with age and later reached out to African Americans, who helped his reelection as governor in 1982. Fear and prejudices can be overcome.

Unanswerable Questions

Challenges to the possibility of peace will likely come in the form of theoretical questions, such as, "Nuclear warheads are about to rain down on major American cities. So how do you apply nonviolence now?" The answer is, "You can't." I like to use the powder keg analogy. You get a barrel, fill it with gunpowder, light the fuse, let it burn down 99 percent, then ask someone how to prevent the explosion. Preventive measures need to be initiated well ahead of that point. The question needs to be reframed as, "What could have started earlier that would have prevented this situation from developing now?"

Condescension

The last obstacle I list is the "X Factor": ourselves. If we pursue peace with an arrogant, "holier than thou" attitude, we will undermine our own cause. This applies whether we are criticizing the other side or condemning those who are not as pure as ourselves. Just as the United States needs to be more humble in world affairs, we individually need to have a certain degree of humility in promoting our cause. When we are trying to draw people in, nothing pushes them away more than condescension.

Selling Peace

It's not enough to call for peace. You must have a plan to achieve it and be able to sell the idea. Professor George Lakoff has documented how conservatives are much more effective than liberals in stating their case, and he has proposed a number of ideas that can be used for selling peace:

- Present your argument in patriotic terms, rather than attacking America for being evil.
- Address political values. There is a lot of overlap between conservative and liberal values; seek areas of agreement in those areas first and then move on to the tougher stuff.
- Passionately frame the issue in your own terms, not theirs; for example, refer to "accrued benefits" rather than "entitlements." If someone says the government is proposing "death panels," point out how the insurance

industry makes life and death decisions about us all the time.

- Always state things in the positive. "Don't do it" sounds like "do it" to the subconscious mind. As an example, a football coach should refer to "ball control" rather than "avoidance of fumbling." Be "pro-peace" rather than "anti-war."

- Remember that *values*, not *programs*, win the vote. State the moral basis for your position. Conservatives talk in terms of "family values," which is vague but appealing. Liberals argue for programs like single-payer health care, without talking about the values behind the program, such as fairness or human dignity. As such, the argument misses its full punch.

- Telling a story gets a message across more vividly and with greater effect than spouting facts or opinions.

- Teach the children. Youthful minds absorb information exceedingly fast. If, in school and at home, we teach our kids the principles of peace—kindness, empathy, compassion—then when they grow up, maybe they will join the movement for a more peaceful world, dragging doubters along with them.

- Have your elevator speech prepared: give your main point in fifteen or twenty seconds. What are your three main arguments for peace?

- Appeal to one's pocketbook. We might prefer that Americans have an overnight spiritual awakening against the immorality of war, but it's probably not going to happen that way. At least right now, people are more likely to be motivated by economic stress than by moral arguments.

8. OUR CHALLENGE

Act locally and pull government along in the process.
—Jeffrey D. Sachs, international development economist

THINKING ABOUT A NEW national security policy and our role in a Great Turning can be daunting. But there are things we can do to put ourselves personally in alignment with the big picture. I have a few suggestions.

Redefine Success and Happiness
Our current standard of living involves having lots of stuff. It also includes working long hours, being stressed, eating food on the run, living beyond our means, worrying about retirement, and not having enough time with family. If a lower standard of living means just having fewer things, that's one thing. But if it means having greater control over your life; feeling more secure; and having a stronger tie with family, neighbors, and community, then we are talking about a higher quality of life.

Given the uncertainty about the future, this is a good time to see life through a new lens and reevaluate what brings us success and happiness. These are some ideas to consider:

1. Learn to be satisfied with sufficiency rather than maximum gain. As we increase our wealth, we supposedly

get happier. However, once our basic survival needs are met and we achieve a degree of comfort and even a few luxuries, we enter a state of excess in which fulfillment, defined as satisfaction or happiness, is likely to decrease. Past the point of "enough," wealth can actually become a burden and get in the way of finding meaning in life (see Figure 14).

2. Appreciate the quality rather than the quantity of things. Having a few nice things can be more fulfilling than having a lot of ordinary possessions.

3. Find gratitude in our hearts for all that is right in the world rather than fretting over everything that is wrong, and express it to others.

4. As hard as it may be, go beyond anger and forgive those who perpetuate and participate in violence and destruction. The first draft of this book was filled with resentment as I felt my country had let me down. Upon rereading it, I realized how much anger I had to let go of to develop a positive message in this book.

5. Given that what we see defines our reality, it wouldn't hurt to unplug, at least somewhat, from the violence that pervades the news media, TV, and movies. The violent imagery in our mass media creates a more violent mind-set, which can lead to more acceptance of violent behavior.

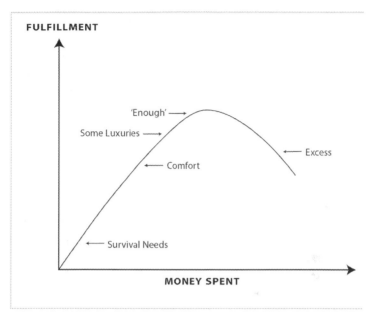

Figure 14. Fulfillment curve. There's a sweet spot in spending, beyond which our sense of fulfillment diminishes.

Develop Community

In the future, the American ethic of rugged individualism will need to give way to a culture of collaboration and community. We will have to rely more on each other than on corporate America to provide for our basic needs such as food, energy, housing, and transportation. The previously discussed Transition movement is working to achieve this end. While not directly a peace movement, it is part of the necessary change needed in this rapidly changing world to create a more fulfilling, equitable, and peaceful society. If there is such a movement in your community, check it out and become active in it. If there isn't, talk to others about starting one. In any event, look for ways to participate in activities that promote mutual support and cooperation in your community: shop at the local farmer's market, join a community-supported agriculture (CSA) program, or wean yourself away from Amazon and shop at the local bookstore. When you shop, be conscious of how and where the product came from.

Serve Others

Once our basic survival needs are met, the primary force driving us all is the need for a higher meaning and purpose in life. Helping another individual or dedicating yourself to a cause can bring great fulfillment. Take action, no matter how insignificant it seems, to serve those around you. Even small acts of love and caring can have ripple effects far beyond what we are able to see. You will be influencing others more than you know. There are many opportunities to serve others in our personal lives if we look for them: dealing with a belligerent boss, competing for a parking place, helping a son or daughter deal with a drug problem.

In the words of Albert Schweitzer, "I don't know what your destiny will be, but I know that the ones among you who will be really happy are those who have sought and found how to serve."

Visualize Peace

We cannot accomplish what we cannot envision. So practice this meditation exercise: Get comfortable and close your eyes, and then think about what an ideal world might look like. Include yourself in the picture. When done, share your vision with others. Here are some teasers:

- Have wars virtually ceased?
- Have nukes disappeared from the face of the Earth?
- Are Israelis and Palestinians living peacefully together?
- Are nonviolence and empathy taught in schools?
- Has hunger been eliminated worldwide?
- Has the world learned to use less oil?
- Are you working fewer hours with more satisfaction?
- Have conservatives, progressives, and libertarians united in a common dream?
- Have our politicians become statesmen?
- Has Fox TV gone liberal and fired Rush Limbaugh?

If we redefine success and happiness, work to develop community, find ways to serve others, and visualize a peaceful future, we can accelerate the transformation to a more peaceful world and help create a new story to take the place of the old.

Story 15. Gross National Happiness

Some economists believe that measuring wealth solely in monetary terms skews government policy to favor greed and consumption. Perhaps we need to change our definition of wealth. An interesting example is found in the nation of Bhutan, a small Tibetan country wedged between India and China. In 1972, its benevolent king adopted Gross National Happiness (GNH) to replace GDP as his country's top priority, measured by 1) equitable socioeconomic development, 2) preservation of cultural values, 3) conservation of the natural environment, and 4) establishment of good governance.

Since then, Eric Weiner, in *The Geography of Bliss: One Grump's Search for the Happiest Places in the World*, reports that Bhutan has had impressive improvements in its standard of living: life expectancy has risen from forty-seven to sixty-six years, the number of people with access to safe drinking water has risen from 45 to 75 percent, and adult literacy has increased from 23 to 54 percent. The country provides free health care and education, and there are more monks than soldiers. While the experience of Bhutan may not be fully exportable, their experience is worth our attention.

The country's success was inspiring enough for British Prime Minister Tony Blair to propose a national index similar to Bhutan's, inserting happiness skills into school curricula and encouraging a better balance between work and family life. While his proposal was never adopted, an organization in London called the New Economics Foundation developed the idea further. They created a measure of human well-being and degree of environmental impact called the Happy Planet Index, defined this way:

$$\text{Happy Planet Index} = \frac{\text{life satisfaction} \times \text{life expectancy}}{\text{ecological footprint}}$$

This index uses quantifiable indicators such as school graduation rates, the percentage of locally owned businesses, the divorce rate, and emissions of CO_2 in the calculation. In 2009, the number one ranked country was Costa Rica. The United States placed 114 out of 143 countries, slightly ahead of Rwanda and Uganda.

Follow Your Passion

Find and follow your own passion. The transition to peace will come from many directions; there is no one role you have to fulfill. You will be most successful doing what you love most, whether it's writing, organizing, doing stand-up comedy, or whatever. People who have relentlessly pursued their passion have started the most successful businesses. The fire in your belly is what drives you forward, willing to overcome any obstacles to achieve your dream. For me, it has been the search for peace. It started during my work in the defense industry and has continued to this day.

Encourage your kids to follow their passions as well. They have an entire life ahead of them to make a difference in the world. They will do it best by doing what they love. Of course, it's not always easy to follow this advice. When I told both my sons to follow their passion, one of them said he wanted to study dramatic arts in college. My reply was, "Wait, I didn't mean *that*!" I had to let go and let him attend drama school, which he did. There he learned stage lighting and he is now successfully and happily working in the commercial lighting business.

9. STIRRING THE EMBERS

Transitioning to peace, one American at a time.

IF YOU LIKE THIS peace message, I have bad news for you. It will not happen, at least not on its own. The good news is that change is already happening. Amid all the war, despair, and suffering in the world, there are indications that the future can be better than the past. As people with free will, we can be whatever we want to be—there is no set course we have to follow. Whether we move in a positive or negative direction is up to us.

Reasons for Optimism

There are three primary reasons I am optimistic about the prospects for peace. First, our country is founded on strong constitutional values. In the second sentence of the Declaration of Independence, Thomas Jefferson wrote, "We hold these truths to be self-evident, that all men are created equal, that they are endowed by their Creator with certain inalienable Rights, that among these are Life, Liberty, and the pursuit of Happiness."

This statement established the high moral principles of a country that was beginning an experiment in government based on freedom, democracy, and rule of the people. Our country was imperfect when it was founded, but it was established on principles that are profound and that continue to guide our way toward becoming a more perfect union.

Second, people are dissatisfied with our dysfunctional, expensive government. In one way or another, I think we are all uncomfortable with our country's direction. We may have different ideas about where to go, but in simplified terms, doves on the Left want less warmongering and more social services, while hawks on the Right want greater national security through American imperial strength. However the dissatisfaction is expressed, the door is opening to reexamine who we are, how we operate, and in what direction we are going. We often see those who view life differently from our own perspective as wrong, unpatriotic, and downright dangerous. We need to open our hearts and minds to jointly find our way forward.

Third, the Millennial Generation is coming along to take over leadership positions in business, government, and the military. Those in their teens and twenties today are the most confident, most environmentally aware, most open to change, and least materialistic of any American generation. In addition to making a livelihood, today's students want to help create a better world. The Millennials get it, and they are the ones who will have to sort all this out.

Takeaway Message

Peace, as I define it, will never come to our planet. There is too much diversity in the human condition to assume that someday all greed, all lust for power, and all mental illness and other aberrations will disappear. As a result, there will always be conflict between people and between nations. The question is how best to avoid those conflicts and resolve them when they occur.

The way of war does not offer a stable path to peace. In fact, it is so unstable that we probably won't have to tear the system down; it may well collapse under its on weight, though in a very messy way. Over time, as our present violent course falters, it will create more insecurity than confidence in people. Serious and obvious cracks will begin to appear in our traditional way of defending ourselves. The

Story 16. Change Is Happening

As evidenced by several recent events, the world is beginning to experience an upheaval in the status quo. The Occupy Wall Street movement is just one part of what is happening around the world.

Latin American Presidents

In the last decade, ten Latin American dictators have been voted out of office, replaced by a new wave of democratically elected presidents who are avoiding debt from the World Bank and are successfully defying the plundering of their country's resources.

In September 2009, seven of these countries started a Bank of the South to finance development projects in agriculture, energy, and health care for member nations. To a large degree, it will replace financing from the World Bank, IMF, and USAID, all organizations that in the past have been the vehicle for other countries to gain control over third world resources.

Arab Spring

In 2011, populist revolts broke out against totalitarian regimes in sixteen Middle East and North African countries. Civil resistance was almost all nonviolent, in the form of strikes, demonstrations, marches, rallies, and the use of social media. They were led mostly by youths who refused to accept the status quo of dictatorships, human rights violations, government corruption, high unemployment rates, and extreme poverty.

The Arab Spring has inspired demonstrations in other countries as well, including the Occupy Wall Street movement in the United States.

American Unions

Unionization, while it has its drawbacks, has historically been a major force in industry and business. But in the last sixty years, union membership in the workforce has declined from roughly 33 percent in 1953 to 12 percent in 2010. Seeing unions as a threat to the corporate world, conservative politicians have recently proposed state legislation to restrict union rights of government workers in Wisconsin, Ohio, Tennessee, and Indiana. In response, union workers and their supporters occupied state capitals and engaged in massive protests. Where laws were passed, recalls were initiated to oust the offending politicians. This was the first show of union strength in decades.

old world views (Left vs. Right, liberal vs. conservative, religious vs. secular, capitalism vs. socialism) will no longer apply. We will need a new way of thinking. Initially at least, it will probably not come from spontaneous, spiritual enlightenment but rather from a concern over worsening economic conditions. Perhaps out of that, we will be able to embrace a new consciousness rooted in a deep connection with the Earth.

This is how I would summarize my views:

Peace Is Possible

When I quit my defense job in protest over forty years ago, I had only a general notion that an alternative to war was possible. The events of 9/11 inspired me to revisit the subject. I have now concluded that while it won't be easy, it is possible to achieve world peace, and in fact, the United States can lead the world toward it. The future will not be the same as the past, and that will open the door for peace to have a chance. Several important things are on our side:

- **Mother Nature** can teach us a lot about how to redesign our society to live in harmony with each other and with the Earth. At the same time, she will remind us when our carelessness and exploitations have gone too far.
- **Economic Principles** will soon catch up with us. Perpetual growth and overconsumption cannot be sustained in a world of finite resources.
- **American Values** are strong and vibrant. At heart, we are a generous people that cherish the values and freedoms that the Founding Fathers placed in the Constitution.

It Can Happen Fast

This is an unprecedented time, given exploding population growth, the impending end of the Oil Age, the effects of climate change, and the fragility of the global economy. Modern terrorism is confounding our Cold War defense structures and draining our federal coffers. A massive change is coming in the years ahead, providing the opportunity for a positive transformation of society, including our military structure.

Given that Americans are intolerant of high taxes, inefficient government, and anything negatively affecting their pocketbook, they may rebel against the high cost of war and demand a reduction in the defense budget that goes far beyond belt tightening. And given the unwillingness of the government to control either our financial system or the national debt, our country could experience the kind of financial crisis that does not allow the military to continue fighting wars, even if it wants to.

Given the rate of change in the world, something resembling world peace could come very rapidly, perhaps in one generation.

We Can Help Make It Happen

Change will not come from a President Gandhi. Given the huge power of large corporations, the military, and defense contractors, change from the top down will be difficult if not impossible. While some support may come from a few brave, enlightened politicians, the initiative for change will come from the bottom up, in different forms. Citizens will be the ones to force politicians to act. All we have to do is put our voices together and get sufficiently organized.

The process will be messy, and things will almost certainly get worse, probably much worse, before they get better. But I have great faith in the upcoming Millennial Generation to see a new path and have the courage and ambition to take us there. With all its shortcomings, America's democracy is what makes our country so resilient and enduring. Ultimately, change will come from the ingenuity, compassion, and ability of the American people to self-correct and chart a more secure and sustainable course for the future.

Take a moment to relax and absorb your sense of this book. Do any of these ideas grab you? What's your biggest argument for peace being possible? What's your greatest counterargument? And given that the solution to one problem can relate to another, how do the Peace Principles and Peace Programs relate to your main issue?

Finally, take another look at the three questions asked in the Introduction.

- **Does our current defense system make you feel safe?**
- **Is it worth the cost?**
- **Is there an alternative to war, and can you help make it happen?**

All I ask is that you think about it.

AFTERWORD

My days of working in the defense industry are long gone. War didn't make sense to me then, and it is still not healthy for children and other living things. Ten years of research deepen my belief that peace is possible. It's never too late to begin doing the right thing, and I have tried to outline what that might look like.

The recent rise of the Occupy Movement makes me hopeful that a sea change in American politics is arriving and that the next generation will create a more peaceful nation that can lead the world away from war. Ninety nine percent of the US population constitutes over 300 million citizens. The remaining admittedly powerful but relatively few, cannot withstand the will of the people forever.

As I think of my sons Gabe and Josh, I wonder if those of our younger generation will have their defining moment. Will they break through centuries of war and find a way to peace? And will we take action now to give them that chance? If we all play our part, the transition to peace may come sooner than anyone could have imagined.

ABOUT THE AUTHOR

Russ Faure-Brac has an MS degree from Stanford University in engineering economics. He previously worked at Stanford Research Institute, where he conducted research on aerospace and weapons systems. The events of September 11, 2001, reawakened his interest in peace, and after ten years of study, he concluded that there is a viable alternative to war and began promoting his message. Now retired, he is active with both the peace and Transition movements and lives with his wife on a small horse ranch in Northern California.

For more information, visit his website at transitiontopeace.com.

SELECTED REFERENCES

This is a list of resources that were particularly useful in my research. A few notes are added about the content of each.

Caldicott, Dr. Helen. *The New Nuclear Danger,* New York Press, 2002.
A feisty doctor documents US buildup of nuclear weapons and warns against the threat of nuclear conflict.

Carter, Jimmy. *Palestine: Peace Not Apartheid,* Simon & Schuster, 2006.
The former president presents a controversial blueprint for bringing peace to Israel and justice to Palestine.

Chomsky, Noam. *Imperial Ambitions,* Metropolitan Books, 2005.
A renowned and outspoken political activist critiques US policies post 9/11.

Chopra, Deepak. *Peace Is the Way,* Harmony Books, 2005.
Citing a Gandhian phrase, Deepak presents a seven-step program to become a true peacemaker.

Clarke, Richard. *The Scorpion's Gate,* G. P. Putnam's Sons, 2005.
A terrorism expert writes a fascinating novel about a Saudi Arabian coup and the avoidance of a possible nuclear war.

Diamond, Jared. *Collapse,* Penguin Books, 2005.
A Pulitzer Prize-winning author documents how environmental abuses have caused the collapse of historic civilizations and how the United States can choose a different path.

Easwaran, Eknath. *Nonviolent Soldier of Islam: Badshah Kahn, A Man to Match His Mountains*, Nilgiri Press, 1999.
Ghaffar Badshah Kahn formed the world's first nonviolent army out of formerly fierce, violent Pathans and defeated repeated brutal attacks from the British. Inspiring reading.

Foell, Earl W. and Richard A. Nenneman. *How Peace Came to the World,* MIT Press, 1986.
A high school contest yielded thirty stories of how nuclear threat and war could vanish by 2010. Fascinating, imaginative reading.

Hartmann, Thom. *Rebooting the American Dream*, Berrett-Koehler, 2010.
A prolific writer argues that the way forward is to look back at the operating system designed by our Founding Fathers.

Heckler, Richard Strozzi. *In Search of the Warrior Spirit,* North Atlantic Books, 1992.
As he teaches Green Berets to live warrior virtues, an aikido instructor struggles with whether he is supporting or converting a fighting machine.

Heinberg, Richard. *The End of Growth*, New Society, 2011.
Heinberg lays out a convincing argument that economic growth is unsustainable and both the Left and the Right miss this point. He then proposes how to build a new economy.

Hopkins, Rob. *The Transition Handbook,* Green Books, 2008.
War results from how societies are formed. Hopkins proposes how creating self-sustaining local communities can transform our society.

Johnson, Chalmers. *Nemesis: Last Days of the American Republic,* Metropolitan Books, 2006.
The final volume of the Blowback Trilogy shows how imperial overstretch is undermining the United States economically and politically.

Keen, Sam. *Faces of the Enemy,* Harper and Row, 2009.
Keen examines the use of propaganda to dehumanize the enemy (available from author Keen only).

Korten, David C. *The Great Turning,* Kumarian Press and Berrett-Koehler, 2006.
The cofounder of the Positive Futures Network argues that empire is not inevitable and details a grassroots strategy for reordering human society.

Korten, David C. *Agenda for a New Economy,* Berrett-Koehler, 2009.
After the 2008 economic meltdown, Korten wrote this book about the unthinkable idea of replacing Wall Street with a new economic model based on real wealth.

Krugman, Paul. *The Great Unraveling,* W. W. Norton, 2003.
An award-winning economist chronicles how the boom economy unraveled and fiscal responsibility collapsed.

Makhijani, Arjun. *Carbon-Free and Nuclear-Free: A Roadmap for U.S. Energy Policy,* IEER Press, 2007. Cogent arguments for weaning ourselves from fossil fuels and nuclear power.

Martenson, Chris. *The Crash Course*, John Wiley & Sons, 2011.
Economic researcher Martenson analyzes the US economy and concludes that we are headed for a crash. He also offers practical advice on how to prepare for it.

McCarthy, Colman. *I'd Rather Teach Peace,* Orbis Books, 2007.
The director of the Center for Teaching Peace writes a charming book about establishing peace studies programs in our schools to teach nonviolence and conflict resolution.

Millman, Dan. *Peaceful Warrior Collection,* MJF Books: a compilation of *Way of the Peaceful Warrior,* 1984, and *Sacred Journey of the Peaceful Warrior,* 1991.
An engaging story of a champion athlete as he learns the life of a warrior.

Mollison, Bill. *Permaculture: A Designer's Manual,* Tagari Publications, 2004.
Chapter 14 applies permaculture principles to strategies for creating an alternative, sustainable political system.

Mortensen, Greg. *Three Cups of Tea*, Penguin Books, 2006.
Getting lost in the mountains of Pakistan leads a climber to establish schools, especially for girls, in the area that gave birth to the Taliban. Forget his recent problems. This is an inspiring read.

Nagler, Michael. *The Search for a Nonviolent Future,* Inner Ocean, 2004.
A peace scholar documents the successful use of nonviolence in the past and shows how nonviolence is an effective solution to political and moral turmoil in the world.

Paige, Glenn D. *Nonkilling: Global Political Science,* Center for Global Nonkilling, 2009.
Paige presents alternative concepts for developing a society in which there is no killing and offers reasons why a nonkilling society is possible.

Perkins, John. *Confessions of an Economic Hit Man,* Berrett-Koehler, 2004.
If you want to know how the real world works, read Perkins's book on how the United States covertly uses rigged elections, payoffs, extortion, sex, and murder to dominate the globe.

Reich, Robert B. *After-Shock: The Next Economy and America's Future,* Alfred A. Knopf, 2010.
Addressing the current economic crisis, the former secretary of labor lays out a blueprint for restoring America's economy and rebuilding our society.

Roy, Arundhati. *An Ordinary Person's Guide to Empire,* South End Press, 2004.
This diminutive, charismatic New Delhi essayist uses humor, impeccable logic, and sharp one-liners to argue that the United States is by no means a great nation, but it could be a great people.

Solomon, Norman. *War Made Easy,* John Wiley & Sons, 2005.
A nationally syndicated columnist and media critic analyzes how the media uses "perception management" techniques to promote American wars.

Twist, Lynn. *The Soul of Money,* W. W. Norton, 2003.
Having trouble with your relationship to money and how it relates to quality of life? Read this book.

Van Gelder, Sarah. *This Changes Everything: Occupy Wall Street and the 99 Percent Movement,* Berrett-Koehler, 2011.
Van Gelder and the staff of *Yes!* magazine describe with great enthusiasm the rise of the Occupy movement and its potential to alter the conversation about American politics and the economy.

Weiner, Eric. *The Geography of Bliss,* Twelve Books, 2008.
A grumpy writer travels through ten countries to find if any of them are happy and, if so, why. A fun read.

Winograd, Morley and Michael Hais. *Millennial Momentum: How a New Generation Is Remaking America*, Rutgers University Press, 2011.
The authors present their research describing the upcoming generation and its potential to define the future.

Younger, Stephen M. *Endangered Species: How We Can Avoid Mass Destruction and Build a Lasting Peace,* Harper Collins, 2007.
A former nuclear weapons researcher proposes a combination of diplomacy, economic measures, and a redefined military capability to achieve national security. An excellent book.

Zinn, Howard. *A People's History of the United States,* Harper Collins, 2003.
American history classes taught us about life from one perspective. Now read America's story from the perspective of women, factory workers, minorities, and the working poor—an eye opener.

BUMPER STICKERS FOR WAR

"Give war a chance."
"I'd rather be water boarding."
"The beatings will continue until morale improves."
"Thou shalt not kill, unless it's in very large numbers."
"Total destruction in thirty minutes or the next one is free."
"When it absolutely, positively has to be destroyed overnight."
"There is no problem that cannot be solved by the use of high
explosives."
"We don't like collateral damage, but it helps if you stay the
@j#$% out of our way."

BUMPER STICKERS FOR PEACE

"Arms are for hugging."
"Real men don't use nukes."
"There is no war to end all wars."
"I'm already against the next war."
"Conflict is inevitable but war is not."
"Peace is the only battle worth waging."
"God bless the whole world, no exceptions."
"There was never a good war or a bad peace."
"You can't kill, jail, or occupy all your enemies."
"We are making enemies faster than we can kill them."
"Terrorism is the war of the poor and war is the terrorism of
the rich."
"When the power of love overcomes the love of power, we'll
have peace."
"You can bomb the world to pieces but you can't bomb the
world to peace."
"Why do we kill people who kill people to show that killing
people is wrong?"
"War is so OVER."
"The times already have changed, Bob."

OPEN BOOK EDITIONS
A BERRETT-KOEHLER PARTNER

Open Book Editions is a joint venture between Berrett-Koehler Publishers and Author Solutions, the market leader in self-publishing. There are many more aspiring authors who share Berrett-Koehler's mission than we can sustainably publish. To serve these authors, Open Book Editions offers a comprehensive self-publishing opportunity.

A Shared Mission

Open Book Editions welcomes authors who share the Berrett-Koehler mission—Creating a World That Works for All. We believe that to truly create a better world, action is needed at all levels—individual, organizational, and societal. At the individual level, our publications help people align their lives with their values and with their aspirations for a better world. At the organizational level, we promote progressive leadership and management practices, socially responsible approaches to business, and humane and effective organizations. At the societal level, we publish content that advances social and economic justice, shared prosperity, sustainability, and new solutions to national and global issues.

Open Book Editions represents a new way to further the BK mission and expand our community. We look forward to helping more authors challenge conventional thinking, introduce new ideas, and foster positive change.

For more information, see the Open Book Editions website:
http://www.iuniverse.com/Packages/OpenBookEditions.aspx

Join the BK Community! See exclusive author videos, join discussion groups, find out about upcoming events, read author blogs, and much more!
http://bkcommunity.com/